St. Barnabas

St. Barnabas

A NOVEL

JOHN SAGER

Inspiring Voices®

Inspiring Voices books may be ordered through booksellers or by contacting:

Inspiring Voices
1663 Liberty Drive
Bloomington, IN 47403
www.inspiringvoices.com
1 (866) 697-5313

ISBN: 978-1-4624-1257-0 (sc)
ISBN: 978-1-4624-1258-7 (e)

Library of Congress Control Number: 2019901911

Print information available on the last page.

Inspiring Voices rev. date: 2/20/2019

Also by John Sager

A Tiffany Monday - - An Unusual Love Story, WestBow Press, 2012

Joan's Gallery, 50 Years of Artistry by Joan Kohl Johnson Sager, Blurb, Inc., 2013

Uncovered - - My Half-Century with the CIA, WestBow Press, 2013

Night Flight, A Novel, Create Space, 2013

Operation Night Hawk, A Novel, Create Space, 2014

Moscow at Midnight, A Novel, Create Space, 2014

The Jihadists' Revenge, A Novel, Create Space, 2014

Mole, A Novel, Create Space, 2015

Capital Crises, A Novel, Create Space, 2015

God's Listeners, An Anthology, Create Space, 2015

Crescent Blood, A Novel, Create Space, 2016

Sasha, from Stalin to Obama, A Biography, Create Space, 2016

Shahnoza – Super Spy, A Novel, Create Space, 2016

Target: Oahu, A Novel, Create Space, 2017

Aerosol, A Novel, Create Space, 2017

The Health Center, A Novel, Create Space, 2017

The Conservator, A Biography, Create Space, 2017

The Evil Alliance, A Novel, Create Space, 2018

Tehran Revisited, A Novel, Archway Publishing, 2019

The Caravan, A Novel, Archway Publishing, 2019

Acknowledgments

Most of my research for this novel has come from various online resources, the Google/Wikipedia combination being the most helpful and oft-used.

There is one other that deserves mention.

The two-volume *The Bible Knowledge Commentary*, authored by John F. Walvoord and Roy B. Zuck. Its New Testament volume contains an extensive exposition (written by Zane C. Hodges) that attributes the writing of *The Letter to the Hebrews* to Barnabas. That exposition begins at page 777 and offers many ideas to support a Barnabas authorship.

And I wish to add a word of thanks to my beautiful step-daughter, Janice Bornstein. A super Christian mom and grandmother, she has perused every page and has made a number of helpful suggestions.

John Sager
Winter 2019

Preface

Historians and archeologists tell us that the first signs of human habitation on the island of Cyprus date to about 10,000 B.C. These were hunter-gatherers who left behind the earliest-known water wells, dug to depths of some two hundred feet. The remarkably well-preserved Neolithic village of Khirokitia is a UNESCO World Heritage Site, dating to approximately 6800 BC.

From Wikipedia, the Free Encyclopedia: *The island is at a strategic location in the Middle East. It was ruled by Assyria for a century starting in 708 BC, before a brief spell under Egyptian rule and eventually Persian rule in 545 BC. The Cypriots, led by Onesilus king of Salamis, joined their fellow Greeks in the Ionian period during the unsuccessful Ionian Revolt in 499 BC. The revolt was suppressed, but Cyprus managed to maintain a high degree of autonomy and remained oriented towards the Greek world.*

And we know that first century Cyprus was one of the Roman empire's far-flung colonies. There is little evidence, however, that Rome chose to interfere with the island's management.

Turning to The New Testament, one finds at least eight references to the island, by name, including the important notation that Barnabas (known then as Joseph) was a Cypriot Jew, that he was well-known there and always a welcome visitor.

This fact of Scripture supports the various themes that appear in this novel.

John Sager
Winter 2019

One

Her final resting place was a shallow one, the two grave diggers finding the rocky soil nearly impenetrable. The body, wrapped in the traditional white linen sheet, was slowly lowered into the grave by his two closest friends. As the earth was returned, one shovelful at a time, the rabbi began reading from the ancient Psalter, followed by the covenant words *May God comfort you among all the mourners of Zion and Jerusalem.*

The mourners then walked the few steps to the synagogue, went inside, sat and listened to rabbi Othonis as he delivered a brief eulogy. His message was simple and brief: How could the God of Our Fathers allow this beautiful, innocent young mother to perish while delivering her first child? Surely there must be an explanation. He urged his congregation to seek answers through fervent prayer.

⁂

The next morning, Costas spoke with the attending midwife. She was beside herself with grief as she tried to explain what had happened:

"Honestly, Sire, there was nothing I could do. As soon as her water broke it was followed by a massive hemorrhaging, more blood than I've ever seen. She died almost immediately, and I know she did not suffer."

"And the child, my son?"

"It's a miracle, Sire! He's as perfect an infant as I've ever seen: black hair, deep brown eyes and - - -"

"And how is he to be fed?"

"I believe God is on our side, Sire. You may remember that only ten days ago I helped deliver a baby girl. The mother is breast feeding her as we speak and I do believe your son can share that gift."

"Very well, and thank you. I expect you to continue caring for my son as long as necessary. As soon as he is able to handle solid food you may return him to me."

⌾⫘⫘⌾

He wouldn't admit it to anyone, but the death of his wife made him wonder if his own life was worth living. But of course it was because now he had a beautiful infant son to care for. With that decision behind him he agreed to the rabbi's naming ceremony, to be followed by circumcision on the eighth day.

Still, he was a troubled man. How could God possibly allow such a terrible thing to happen? Everyone understood that the human body was a mystery and those few who dared to claim an understanding of it were rarely believed. The more he thought about it the angrier he became. Worse, his anger had begun to interfere with his work. It wasn't fair but he couldn't help himself.

⚬⚬⚬

"Loukas, will you never learn!? For the third time I'm telling you, you *cannot* use that draw knife to reshape that piece of wood! It's oak and it's too hard."

"Yes, Sire, I know. But Elias has borrowed my sharpening stone and he has not yet returned it. When he does, I'll be able to hone my knife so that it *will* reshape that piece. And, as you know, Sire, sharpening stones are very expensive. We have only two of them for our entire crew."

"When will he return it?"

"He promised, no later than tomorrow."

"Very well. But if he does not return it tomorrow, you tell me. I needn't remind you that we *must* finish construction of this ship before the weather turns bad, probably no more than two months hence."

⚬⚬⚬

Costas walked from the water's edge up the long grade to his sheltered work bench, pulled up his stool, sat down and began to calculate. His small company's contract called for the ship to be finished *before* the spring rains began. At five thousand drachmas he would barely make a profit. Worse, the contract required him to find and train the twenty oarsmen who would be powering the ship. Yes, it would have a sail, but the Great Sea's winds were unreliable.

Then, there was the significant issue of below-deck storage. The ship's maiden voyage was to haul fifty barrels of pure olive oil, from its launching skids at the harbor's edge all the way to the eastern shore of The Great Sea, a distance of four thousand stadia. The barrels were being crafted by a friend of Costas, he was almost on schedule and, as the gods would have it, olive oil does not spoil if the barrels are tightly sealed.

And when would he receive his five thousand drachmas? Only *after* the fifty barrels had been received and counted. This good news would return to him on another ship so that Costas would wait at least six months before receiving payment. Fortunately for him, he had other things to do. While his ship was making it way across The Great Sea, he would finish the work on the town's new synagogue, a project he much preferred to building ships.

⌘

The still-grieving Costas found some comfort by attending services at the town's only synagogue. It helped that the rabbi was a good friend and he enjoyed listening to him as he read from a priceless papyrus scroll every Saturday evening—tales of Moses and the burning bush, of patriarch Abraham's promise from *Yahweh Elohim* that his offspring would count as the sands of the seashore. Despite his skepticism, he felt obliged to be there, every week, and he promised himself that his infant son Joseph—who would never enjoy a mother's love—would join him in a few more years.

⌘

The old synagogue had been destroyed by fire and the townspeople could only stand and watch. The nearest water supply was a five-minute walk and there were only ten watertight animal skins with which to carry water. The Paphos Elder Council agreed that the new synagogue should be built on the site of the old one, which meant that the same dirt track would allow people to come by horse cart or walk, whichever they preferred.

And there had been a few complaints from the town's women. They were accustomed to attending the synagogue with the *mechitzah* separating them from the men, always at the rear of the hall where it was nearly impossible to hear the rabbi's words. But in the new synagogue, they argued, the mechitzah should be placed much closer to the front of the building.

After listening to them, Costas agreed that their complaint was valid. He returned to his drawing board and sketched in the new location of the mechitzah. Then he rounded up his three-man crew of carpenters, showed them the sketches and put them to work.

Their first task was to take a large horse cart into the nearby pine forest. Many of those trees had stopped growing years before and the wood had self-cured. After bringing them back to the construction site, the logs had to be peeled, notched and hammered into place with iron spikes; then the gaps sealed with an adhesive mixture of wet clay and sawdust. While that was being done, Costas returned to his workshop and found what he knew had to be there: *glass* window panes, purchased only six months ago from a cargo vessel that had stopped at his port for minor repairs. He'd kept this a secret because glass was unheard of until recently when a passing ship captain told him about it. Previously, throughout the island, the windows of buildings and homes were fitted with specially-treated animal hides, to allow some natural light into the rooms, while providing a barrier to insects.

Three months later, to the very day, the new synagogue was complete. At rabbi Othonis' suggestion, the townsfolk organized a celebration, highlighted by the presence of a new batch of red wine, harvested, pressed, aged for three years and then saved for a special occasion.

⁕

The following Sunday, Costas hitched up his horse cart and began the arduous journey northeast across the island to the village of Salamis, nearly 4,000 stadia distant. He was thankful that ten years earlier a company of Roman soldiers had arrived, determined to control the island's restive population. They were there long enough to decide the island needed a paved road, to replace the deeply-rutted dirt tracks that crisscrossed the island. They laid down paving stones the entire distance, but even with the paving stones it would require four days.

Costas had done this before and he knew that if he carried four large loaves of bread, a leather pouch full of sheep sausage and a large porcelain cup with which to dip water from the many streams, he believed he could arrive safely. His hired man Antonos would be expecting him because it was his habit to visit his orchards two times each year. Antonos had been tending the orchards ever since they were planted, some fifteen years earlier. Now was harvest time and both men would work together for the next week, or more, if necessary, to pick and package the oranges and other citrus. It was hard work and a very short season but fresh citrus demanded a high price throughout the island's markets. If any was left over, it would be sold to the next vessel that stopped at the Salamis port.

※

After he returned to his home, Costas reviewed his labors over the preceding six months. He was becoming a wealthy man, perhaps the most wealthy man on the island. And that was exactly what he wanted, a large inheritance to pass on to his only child, Joseph.

Two

It was understood that, at least once each year, a ship would arrive in the harbor—bringing with it letters, a few immigrating Greek citizens, and word-of mouth news from the eastern shores of The Great Sea. Costas anticipated these infrequent visits with great anticipation. His brother lived in a place known to him only as Caesarea, apparently the only port with a decent harbor, merchants, shops and traders.

So it was that one of these ships arrived at the island's harbor at eventide, with just enough daylight remaining for the ship's crew and its oarsmen to come ashore and seek food and overnight shelter. Early the next morning, Costas and many of his friends sought the captain of the ship to learn if he carried news or letters from Caesarea and the neighboring villages.

Yes, he had three letters, one addressed to Costas. The letter was written on a small papyrus scroll, wrapped and sealed in a waterproof sea otter's skin. Costas accepted the letter, returned to his quarters and read it.

My dear Brother Costas. I presume you are still alive and well. If not, the reader of this letter may discard it. Life here in Caesarea is good. I have a small business, selling fresh fruit and vegetables to those who are about to embark on ships like the one that brought you this letter. I am told that such foodstuffs are hard to come by where you live. I also trade in precious stones and metal trinkets, some of my customers believe these will bring good luck and avoid the perils of crossing the open ocean.

But my principal purpose in writing is to tell you that my wife recently has given birth to a most robust infant. After much discussion, we decided to name him John Mark, John from my side of the family, Mark from hers. This means that you, my favorite brother, now have a nephew and should you someday have a child, he/she will have a cousin.

Please respond to this letter so that I know you have received it.

Most cordially, your brother Nicos.

⌘

Costas' reaction was one of joy and anticipation. Because infant Joseph could never have a sibling, a cousin would be the next best thing. How long would it be before the two cousins could meet? At the moment they were separated by many stadia of open ocean. But if his prayers to *Yahweh Elohim* were answered, the two cousins, eventually, would be come lifelong friends with a shared mission.

⌘

The surrogate mother returned his son to him in due time. Now, how to raise an infant son, continue his work, supervise his employees—all without a helper? It was no secret that widower Costas was the most eligible bachelor on the island; handsome, wealthy, virile and unattached. Should he marry again? If he did, his son would have a mother and infant Joseph would receive the love and full-time attention that Costas could never provide. He decided to talk to his rabbi friend, Marios Othonis.

"Marios, I have prayed about this but I believe I have not yet received an answer."

"What kind of prayer?"

"It's about my future and the future of my son Joseph."

"What kind of questions?"

"Yahweh Elohim is all-knowing, you know that as well as anyone."

"Yes, of course, but I repeat: What kind of questions?"

"As you know, Joseph no longer has a mother. If I were to marry again, he would have a mother. And I'm asking Yahweh Elohim if He believes this is a good idea."

"Hmmm, perhaps you haven't received an answer because Yahweh Elohim wants you to answer the question yourself."

"In what way?"

"How many women do you know who might be willing to marry you?"

"I have no idea. There aren't that many in our community. What, there are about forty married couples and you and I know every one of them."

"Surely you have not forgotten Alexia. She was widowed only last year when her husband died of the fever. They never had children and now she's working as a housemaid. She's attractive and she has a positive attitude about most things. I know, because I have counseled her."

"Yes, now that you mention it, I do remember her. Would you be willing to arrange an introduction? We could meet in the synagogue and talk about things."

"Yes, of course I can do that. But when you say 'about things,' she will know almost immediately why I have arranged the meeting. Alexia is a bright, young woman. You would be most fortunate if she should agree to be your wife."

⊙〰〰〰⊙

It was a whirlwind courtship, each of the two knowing exactly what was at stake. The attraction between the two was instant and fierce. Alexia was drawn to baby Joseph as much as she was to his father. A month after they were introduced, they were married, rabbi Othonis officiating.

Three

The following six years passed too quickly. Joseph now had baby step-brother Elias, whom he adored, encouraging him to try walking on his own without the help of his mother.

When he was four, Alexia decided her step-son was bright and curious enough to begin to learn how to read and write. He caught on quickly and within a few months was pronouncing words—even phrases sometimes—that he could read from the one papyrus scroll the family had borrowed from the synagogue. The Hebrew texts were at first difficult but he quickly learned to match the letters with sounds. But there was a problem because many of their neighbors spoke Greek, not Hebrew. So little Joseph would have to become bi-lingual if he were to make his way in his new world.

Then Alexia decided it would be safe enough to allow Joseph to go on walks, by himself. She had nothing to fear because the entire community recognized the child as the son of Costas, the town's most influential citizen.

Joseph's favorite walking path took him some distance into the island's forest. He began to recognize the various leaf patterns of the trees and bushes, the spring-time wild flowers. He was alert to the calls of a number of birds and when he returned to his home he asked Alexia if it were possible to jot down his memories on a piece of parchment. Writing was challenge for the four-year-old, but he soon learned how to use the tip of an eagle's feather, dip it into a mixture of powdered charcoal, water and gum. Soon, he had a small collection of drawings: birds and leaves and flowers, with notes to remind himself where and when he had made his observations.

☙

After each evening meal, Costas asked Alexia about his son's progress. It was clear to each of them that they had a budding prodigy in their small family: smart, alert, inquisitive and obedient. But, thought Costas, something was missing.

"What do you think, Alexia, could our son defend himself if the neighborhood boys decided to test him?"

"I don't believe that's ever been an issue. His playmates like him and he likes them. Why do you ask?"

"I remember when I was his age. More than once I had to defend myself, with nothing but my bare fists. When I was older we learned that the Romans had developed a competitive sport. They called it 'boxing' and covered their hands with wraps of cloth. Depending on the nature of the contest, it could become a deadly event."

"Do you intend to teach our son how to do that?"

"Not yet; he's too young. But there *is* something I'd like to teach him and I should do it before the weather turns colder.

☙

Three weeks later, at the edge of the nearby river.

"What are we doing here, Father? You haven't explained."

"No, Joseph, I haven't. But I'm about to."

"Yes?"

"As you know, Son, we live on an island. You also know that the only way to come to the island, or to leave it, is by ship. And sometimes these ships have problems. The Great Sea's weather can change quickly. Sometimes these ships haven't been properly constructed and they leak, badly enough that they could sink."

"Has that actually happened?"

"Yes, it has. More than once."

"What happened to the men on the ship?"

"Unfortunately, some of them drowned. But not all."

"Why not all?"

"Because some of them had learned how to *swim*. And that's why we're here. I'm going to teach you how to swim so that you will never have to be afraid of the water.

We'll walk over to that fallen tree, take off our clothes and I'll show you how it's done."

∞

Costas didn't know what to expect. Reluctance, fear, refusal? In knee-deep water he supported his son by holding his body a few centimeters below the river's surface.

"Okay, Joseph, I won't let you sink because I have my hands under your back.. I want you to look straight up into the sky. Take a deep breath and you'll see that you won't sink. You'll float. That's the important first step, to convince yourself that you will not sink as long as you can breathe.

"Now, you turn over and I'll support you with my hands under your chest. You look straight ahead, keep your legs straight and kick. --- Good, that's the idea. Now, I want you to take a deep breath and hold it and I'll lower you into the river. Keep your eyes open and you'll see the river's bottom. When you need to breathe, turn your head sidewise and take a breath."

As Costas had expected, his young son was a quick learner. The following week, the two parents agreed: It was safe enough to let Joseph go to the river by himself, there to practice his newfound skill.

Four

eanwhile, Costas' business had expanded three-fold. His contract for ship-building now required *three* ships every year. To meet this demand he hired another twenty workers, including a sail maker, built a covered shed between the town and the harbor to shelter his log-splitting operation, designed and fabricated a pitch-producing oven and hired a blacksmith who would meet the increasing demand for iron spikes.

Young Joseph, ever curious, persuaded his father to let him watch the frenetic activities. He soon learned the names of all the workers and became a helping hand by bringing them fresh drinking water. It was hard work for the youngster, drawing water from the town's only well and then carrying it in two wooden buckets, attached to a long pole slung across his shoulders.

∽༄∽

Because Costas' shipbuilding program was the town's primary source of income, he felt an obligation to help feed its citizens. There was a parcel of undeveloped land within walking distance of the town's center. Surely it would be suitable for growing wheat or barley, but the soil would have to be cultivated before sowing the seeds. He talked to his blacksmith and the two of them designed an iron plowshare, fitted two wooden handles with a cross-piece, then a twelve-tine harrow and, finally, a harness with which to attach it to a horse.

"Who do you intend to use these tools, Sire?"

"I've been asking that question myself. My son Joseph has a way with animals, they seem to respond to his kindnesses, perhaps he could do it. He's old enough now, nearly fully grown. I'll ask him."

⚬⚬⚬

Joseph, now a strapping eighteen-year-old, became the town's favorite farmer. Two of the town's elders provided the seed, from last year's harvest, and after plowing and harrowing the plot Joseph persuaded three of his young friends to help him sow the seed. They were just in time because the next evening a light rainfall covered the island. Some said it was God's provision, noting that without Joseph it would not have happened.

Within a few weeks, the tender, greet shoots began to appear and Joseph and his friends agreed to a method for watering the field: Every morning, at sunrise, they drew water from the town's well, then transferred the water to a tanned animal hide pouch.

After arriving at the field, the pouch was pricked with a sharp bone needle so that the water flowed out in a fine spray. They repeated the process as often as necessary, until the shoots matured to full-length stalks of wheat and barley.

Meanwhile, Joseph had asked his father for permission to

consult the town's blacksmith. At least two scythes would be needed to cut and gather the stalks. The blacksmith had four of these in his inventory and he sold two of them to Joseph, one drachma for each scythe.

෴

Unbeknownst to Joseph, his father Costas asked the town council to set aside a Friday evening to which would be invited as many citizens who wished to attend. There would be fresh baked bread, made with wheat and barely flour, the wheat and barely from the field that Joseph and his friends had cared for. Also on the menu: fresh orange juice from one of Costas' nearby orchards, grape wine for those who preferred it, roasted sausage, and pine nuts for dessert.

After eating their fill, the party-goers gathered to sing hymns of praise to Yahweh Elohim and Costas read from the Psalter.

The event was a huge success. Everyone said so and rabbi Othonis highlighted it in his sermon the following Saturday morning.

෴

Reflecting on the celebration, Costas had an uneasy feeling. His son Joseph had become the most popular young man on the island but his formal education had come to a standstill. There were no institutions of higher learning on the island and admission to the few trade schools didn't seem to Costas to be what his son needed.

As far as he could recall, none of the island's young men had ever opted for *ministry*. Rabbi Othonis was the exception but he was in his mid-fifties. No, Joseph needed a formal education at a higher level and that could be found only in far-away Jerusalem. Costas had heard of a famous rabbi, Gamaliel. He was reputed to be a great teacher and he was also a member of Jerusalem's Sanhedrin Council, the ruling body over all of Israel.

Two questions: Was Joseph 'good enough' to be accepted by Gamaliel and how much would it cost? The later question could only be answered after the answer to the first. In any case, Costas had amassed a small fortune from his shipbuilding business and the cost would be a minor issue. After informing Joseph, he wrote a letter and had it posted on the next outbound ship.

⌘

Eight weeks later, he received a reply, written and signed by Gamaliel's secretary:

'Greetings from Jerusalem. We have examined carefully your application, noting your son's record of service to his community, his participation in the affairs of your synagogue and the endorsements from neighbors and colleagues which you provided. Our distinguished teacher, Gamaliel, has himself reviewed these qualifications and has accepted your application. Please understand that our next available position for your son's indoctrination will occur six months hence. He should bring with him the enrollment fee, as prescribed below, and be prepared to attend classes for six months.

'Most sincerely, Enzo Mendel, secretary to rabbi Gamaliel.'

⌘

Patience had never been one of Costas' stronger qualities but after waiting for nearly a year, Joseph returned from Jerusalem, a changed man. He was now a certified rabbi, qualified to preach and teach in the town's synagogue. But the best news of all: While in Jerusalem, Joseph had met a man known as Saul of Tarsus. They had become fast friends and promised each other that, some day, they would team together to make a difference in God's world.

Five

oseph now found himself in control of his father's shipbuilding business. Costas had decided, after observing his fiftieth birthday, that it was time to retire. Joseph could manage the business as well as he, perhaps better.

Savvas Georgiou, Joseph's foreman and his most experienced workman, had asked his master if he'd ever considered going to sea in one of his own ships. Were he to do that, he suggested, Joseph would experience what life is really like on one of his vessels. In doing so, he likely would observe some of the small, workaday details that would lead to improvements in the design and construction of the next ship.

It bothered Joseph that he hadn't thought of this himself, so much so that he was having trouble sleeping.

Then late one night he had a dream, or a vision. The message was clear enough: *Joseph, you must board the next vessel to leave the harbor, one that will take you across the Great Sea to Antioch. There, you will find men who want to speak to you.*

On waking that morning Joseph thought that perhaps his dream was just that, only a dream that made no sense. Besides, he was reluctant to leave his shipbuilding business in the hands of someone less qualified that he.

But only twenty four hours later, late at night, he received the same message, the same voice. *Joseph, you must respond as I have directed you. You will not regret it.*

⚬⚬⚬

Six weeks later, Joseph stepped ashore at Seleucia. A man named Simeon met him.

"You are Joseph the shipbuilder?"

"Yes, I am. Who are you?"

"My name is Simeon and I'm one of the men the Holy Spirit told you about, in that vision you had."

"*Holy Spirit?* What does that mean?"

"If you'll come with me you will understand everything."

⚬⚬⚬

Their journey to Antioch was made easier because Simeon had rented a two-wheeled cart, pulled by a horse, with enough room for two passengers. They arrived in Antioch just as the sun was setting. Two men were there to meet them, Lucius and Manaen.

"Brother Joseph, I am called Manaen and I will be your host. I suggest you stay at our modest inn and in the morning we will talk."

"That's fine, but can you tell me why I am here? Your friend Simeon said something about the *Holy Spirit*, and I don't know what that means."

"As I said, in the morning we will talk."

⚬⚬⚬

Joseph found it nearly impossible to sleep, so great was his confusion. But after a breakfast of tea, freshly-baked *Challah* and a slice of goat cheese he was ready. As he was finishing his meal, Manaen appeared in the doorway, accompanied by the same Simeon who had met him in Seleucia.

"Brother Joseph. Good morning, We trust you're well rested and ready to hear what we have to say."

"Perhaps not well rested, but ready, nonetheless."

"Good. We can begin by recalling your experience at your home in far-away Cyprus. You were sleeping and you had what you thought was dream, a dream in which you were told to come here."

"Of course I remember that. And I'll never forget it, something totally unexpected."

"That *voice* you heard was from what we refer to as The Holy Spirit. It is a voice of three persons, God, our Savior Jesus Christ and their spirit, three in one. And, of course, it is indeed a miracle. We cannot fully explain it but we know, for certain, that it is real and that it exists in the hearts of everyone of us who has accepted Jesus Christ.

"And you know that your Prophet Isaiah, four hundred years ago, predicted that your Messiah would someday appear. Also, your prophet Joel spoke of the Holy Spirit. These prophesies have been fulfilled in the person of Jesus Christ and that is why we brought you here, so that you can become one of us.

"And, one more thing. Before Jesus departed from this world He told his followers that we are to be His witnesses, not just in Israel but everywhere. That is why we need your help, Joseph.

"Now, we want to pray and we'll do that by laying our hands on your shoulders. You should pray with us and perhaps you will hear again from the Holy Spirit."

The prayer was audible and it was brief but before Simeon had finished, Joseph again heard that *voice: Joseph, Joseph, I want you and need you. You can accomplish much for My kingdom.*

When Simeon had finished he saw that Joseph had fallen to his knees, tears streaming down his cheeks. He heard Joseph whisper, *Yes, Lord, I believe and I will be Your servant.*

Six

The town of Tarsus hosted two taverns, each within easy walking distance of the other. The one alongside the river was Saul's favorite. If he looked carefully enough he could see the thousands of tiny insects swarming over the water and, occasionally, a large trout would break the surface and inhale its midday meal. He had just finished his second cup of tea when a familiar figure appeared in the doorway.

"Is that really *you*, Joseph!? How long as it been? Two years?"

"Yes, indeed, Brother Saul. It hasn't been easy but I've finally found you. One of the merchants said you might be here, and he was right."

"It's strange, isn't it? Rabbi Gamaliel predicted that we would meet again, and within two years of graduating from his class. But, tell me, what brings you here?"

"Before we get to that, there's something you need to know. I'm no longer known as Joseph. The men in Antioch have given me a new name, Barnabas, something about encouraging others.

"And it's important that you know I only recently visited Antioch. I was told to go there by the Holy Spirit, which at that time made no sense to me. But two men met me—Lucius and Manaen—and after some time they laid their hands on my shoulders and prayed, asking the Holy Spirit to come upon me. I heard a voice that said to me *Joseph, Joseph, I want you and need you. You can accomplish much for My kingdom.* That explains why I now consider myself to have finally accepted Jesus as my Lord and Savior."

⟋⟋⟍⟍

"My Christian brothers asked me to come here, find you, and bring you back to Antioch. You probably haven't heard, but Jerusalem's leaders have refused to accept our gospel message. They ordered us to leave and so we moved to Antioch. The locals there pretty much leave us alone and we're free to preach and teach."

"But why do they—you—want *me?*"

"Simple. Two weeks ago, I was praying with a few of my friends and the Holy Spirit suddenly appeared and told us that we need to begin pushing our movement beyond its present limitations, north to Cilicia, Pamphilia and Pisidia. I can't do it by myself and our brothers decided that you would be the ideal teammate. How soon can you be ready?"

"Ready for what?"

"Ready to be my companion. As I said, I can't do this alone and you're the one person that I and my friends believe should go."

"Well, I won't refuse the request of a good friend, so yes, I'll come with you."

⟋⟋⟍⟍

One week later, after traveling to Antioch, the two men were together with others, Simeon, Lucius and Manaen. While they were praying the Holy Spirit interrupted, telling Saul and Barnabas to prepare themselves for an important mission. As the mission would put the men in contact with Gentiles, Saul decided to use his Roman name, Paul. And, knowing its importance, the others laid their hands on them, prayed and bid them goodbye.

⁓

"That was quite a message, wouldn't you say?"

"Indeed it was, Brother Paul. But I like the idea because we've been directed to go to Cyprus, that's where I grew up, as you know. And I've asked my cousin John Mark to join us. I trust him and I know he'll be a big help."

"Have you ever been to Seleucia? That's where we'll find a ship, one that will take us to Salamis."

"No, never, but I understand there are several ships there, with thirty oarsmen, each. It should take about ten days to get there and it's the captain's duty to be sure there's enough food and water for everyone."

⁓

At Salamis, the team found the town's synagogue and preached the word of God. Because the congregation recognized Barnabas as one of their own, many believed.

Then they preached from town to town across the entire island until finally they reached Paphos where they met a Jewish sorcerer, a dishonest prophet named Bar-Jesus. He had attached himself to the governor, Sergius Paulus, a man of considerable insight and influence. The governor invited Barnabas and Paul to visit him, because he wanted to hear their message from God.

But the sorcerer, Elymas, interfered and urged the governor to pay no attention to what Paul and Barnabas said, trying to keep him from trusting the Lord. Then Paul, filled with the Holy Spirit, glared angrily at the sorcerer and said, "You son of the devil, full of every sort of trickery and villainy, enemy of all that is good, will you never end your opposition to the Lord? And now God has laid his hand of punishment upon you, and you will become blind."

Instantly it became dark, and he began wandering, begging for someone to take his hand and lead him.

When the governor saw what happened, he believed and was astonished at the power of God's message.

⁂

Paul and Barnabas decided they'd done all the could on the island and they found another ship at the port town of Paphos. This one, they knew, would take them to Asia, a place they had never been before, and as they expected, the ship docked at the town of Perga.

Then, once ashore, John Mark told Paul and Barnabas he had decided he wasn't suited for this kind of service. The three men got into a heated argument, nearly forgetting they were Christian friends, but John Mark insisted on having it his way. Then he made arrangements to return to Jerusalem. Before parting, he told Paul and Barnabas he was certain they would meet again, in service for the Lord Jesus.

⚬⚬⚬

Now, Barnabas and Paul had a decision to make: how to move north through a vast wilderness, an area they knew nothing about. Do they hire a horse, or walk? Horses, they knew, were often confiscated by Roman soldiers who claimed they had Caesar's approval to do whatever was necessary to protect the empire.

The two men decided to walk, knowing it would take at least four days to reach Antioch, a city in the province of Pisidia. Paul had heard about this place before, from a friend of his in Jerusalem. He said there were many Jewish men in Antioch and they all belonged to the city's one synagogue.

After walking, sometimes stumbling, for four days, the men were exhausted, nearly too tired to do what they had come to do.

But they found the city's one synagogue and after introducing themselves to the rabbi, they were allowed to sleep inside the building. The next morning, a Saturday, the rabbi provided a modest breakfast of tea and three slices of *matzo*, then he stepped outside to welcome the first of his congregants to arrive. Within the hour all the pews were occupied and the worshippers were surprised to see two strangers, two men who apparently had won the trust of their rabbi.

As was his custom, the rabbi read from the books of Moses and from the prophets, and then spoke directly to Paul and Barnabas.

"Brothers, if you have any word of instruction for us come and give it!"

Then, Paul stood, waved a greeting to them and began.

"Men of Israel, and all others here who reverence God, let me begin my remarks with a bit of history.

"The God of this nation Israel chose our ancestors and honored them in Egypt by leading them out of their slavery. And he nursed them through forty years of wandering in the wilderness. Then he destroyed seven nations in Canaan and gave Israel their land as an inheritance. Judges ruled for about four hundred and fifty years and were followed by Samuel the prophet. Then the people begged for a king, and God gave them Saul, a man of the tribe of Benjamin, who reigned for forty years.

"But God removed him and replaced him with David as king, a man about whom God said, 'David is a man after my own heart, for he will obey me.' And it is one of King David's descendants, Jesus, who is God's promised Savior of Israel!

"But before he came, John the Baptist preached the need for everyone in Israel to turn from sin to God. As John was finishing his work he asked, 'Do you think I am the Messiah? No! But he is coming soon—and in comparison with him, I am utterly worthless.'

"Brothers—you sons of Abraham, and also all of you Gentiles here who reverence God—this salvation is for all of us! The Jews in Jerusalem and their leaders fulfilled prophecy by killing Jesus; for they didn't recognize him or realize that he is the one the prophets had written about, though they heard the prophets' words read every Sabbath.

"They found no just cause to execute him, but asked Pilate to have him killed anyway. When they had fulfilled all the prophecies concerning his death, he was taken from the cross and placed in a tomb. But God brought him back to life again! And he was seen many times during the next few days by the men who had accompanied him to Jerusalem from Galilee—these men have constantly testified to this in public witness.

"And now Barnabas and I are here to bring you this Good News—that God's promise to our ancestors has come true in our own time, in that God brought Jesus back to life again. This is what the second Psalm is talking about when it says concerning Jesus, 'Today I have honored you as my Son.' For God had promised to bring him back to life again, no more to die. This is stated in the Scripture that says, 'I will do for you the wonderful thing I promised David.' In another Psalm he explained more fully, saying, 'God will not let his Holy One decay.' This was not a reference to David, for after David had served his generation according to the will of God, he died and was buried, and his body decayed.

"Brothers! Listen! In this man Jesus there is forgiveness for your sins! Everyone who trusts in him is freed from all guilt and declared righteous—something the Jewish law could never do. But, be careful! Don't let the prophets' words apply to you. For they said, 'Look and perish, you despisers of the truth, for I am doing something in your day—something that you won't believe when you hear it announced.' "

As the people left the synagogue that day, they asked Paul to return and speak to them again the next week. And many Jews and believing Gentiles who worshiped at the synagogue followed Paul and Barnabas down the street as the two men urged them to accept the mercies God was offering.

The following week almost the entire city turned out to hear them preach. But when the Jewish leaders saw the crowds, they became jealous, and cursed and argued against whatever Paul said. Then Paul and Barnabas spoke out boldly and declared, "It was necessary that this Good News from God should be given first to you Jews. But since you have rejected it and shown yourselves unworthy of eternal life—well, we will offer it to Gentiles.

For this is as the Lord commanded when he said, 'I have made you a light to the Gentiles, to lead them from the farthest corners of the earth to my salvation.' "

In this way, God's message spread all through that region. But in retaliation, the Jewish leaders incited a mob against Paul and Barnabas, and ran them out of town.

They decided they'd had enough and moved on, to Iconium.

⁂

As soon as they arrived, Paull and Barnabas went together to the synagogue and preached with such power that many—both Jews and Gentiles—believed. But the Jews who didn't agree persuaded their friends not to trust these two, saying all kinds of bad things about them. Still, they stayed there a long time and God showed how their message was from him by giving them power to do great miracles.

But the people of the city had differing ideas about them. Some agreed with the Jewish leaders, and some agreed with the apostles. But then Paul and Barnabas learned of a plot to incite the local citizens to attack and stone them, they fled for their lives, going to the cities of Lycaonia, Lystra and Derbe.

⁂

While they were at Lystra, in the town's central square, they saw a man with crippled feet who had been that way from birth, and he had never walked. He was listening as Paul preached, and Paul noticed him and thought he probably had enough faith to be healed. So Paul called to him, "Stand up!" and the man leaped to his feet and started walking! When the crowd saw what Paul had done, they shouted, "These men are gods in human bodies!"

But Paul was able to persuade them that they were really human beings, just like the rest of them, but that wasn't enough. Because only a few days later, some Jews arrived from Antioch and Iconium and turned the crowds into an angry mob that stoned Paul and dragged him out of the city, believing he was dead. But—another of God's miracles—he was able to stand up and walk as though nothing had happened. The next day he left with Barnabas for Derbe.

⁂

Along the way, Paul and Barnabas appointed elders in each of the new churches and prayed for them, beseeching God to help them grow and prosper.

Then they traveled back through Pisidia to Pamphylia, preached again in Perga, and went on to Attalia. Finally they returned by ship to Antioch, where their journey had begun and where they had been committed to God for the work now completed.

When they arrived, they called together the believers and reported on their trip, telling how God had opened the door of faith to the Gentiles, too. And they stayed in Antioch for many days.

Seven

While Paul and Barnabas were at Antioch, some men from Judea arrived and began to teach the believers that unless they adhered to the ancient Jewish custom of circumcision, they could not be saved. Paul and Barnabas argued and discussed this with them at length, and finally the believers sent them to Jerusalem, accompanied by some local men, to talk to the apostles and elders there about this question.

After the entire congregation had escorted them out of the city, the delegates went on to Jerusalem, stopping along the way in the cities of Phoenicia and Samaria to visit the believers, telling them that the Gentiles, too, were being converted.

After they arrived, they met with the church leaders—all the apostles and elders were present—and Paul and Barnabas reported on what God had been doing through their ministry. But then some of the men who had been Pharisees before their conversion stood and declared that all Gentile converts must be circumcised and required to follow all the Jewish customs and ceremonies. So the apostles and church elders called for another meeting to decide this question.

At the meeting, after much discussion, Peter stood and addressed them

"Brothers, you all know that God chose me from among you long ago to preach the Good News to the Gentiles so that they also could believe. God, who knows men's hearts, confirmed the fact that he accepts Gentiles by giving them the Holy Spirit, just as he gave him to us. He made no distinction between them and us, for he cleansed their lives through faith, just as he did ours. And now are you going to correct God by burdening the Gentiles with a yoke that neither we nor our fathers were able to bear?

Don't you believe that all are saved the same way, by the free gift of the Lord Jesus?"

There was no further discussion, and everyone now listened as Barnabas and Paul told about the miracles God had done through them among the Gentiles. When they had finished, James, their leader, stood to speak.

"Brothers," he said, "listen to me. Peter has told you about the time God first visited the Gentiles to take from them a people to bring honor to his name. And this fact of Gentile conversion agrees with what the prophets predicted. For instance, listen to this passage from the prophet Amos, God is speaking:

'Afterwards I will return and renew the broken contract with David, so that Gentiles, too, will find the Lord—all those marked with my name.'

That is what the Lord says, who reveals his plans made from the beginning. And so my judgment is that we should not insist that the Gentiles who turn to God must obey our Jewish laws, except that we should write to them to refrain from eating meat sacrificed to idols, from all fornication, and also from eating the meat of strangled animals.

For these things have been forbidden in Jewish synagogues in every city on every Sabbath for many generations."

Then the apostles and elders and the whole congregation voted to send delegates to Antioch with Paul and Barnabas, to report this decision. The men chosen were two of the church leaders—Judas and Silas.

This is the letter they took along with them: "*From:* The apostles, elders and brothers at Jerusalem. "*To:* The Gentile brothers in Antioch, Syria and Cilicia. Greetings!

"We understand that some believers from here have upset you and questioned your salvation, but they had no such instructions from us. So it seemed wise to us, having unanimously agreed on our decision, to send to you these two official representatives, along with our beloved Barnabas and Paul. These men—Judas and Silas, who have risked their lives for the sake of our Lord Jesus Christ—will confirm orally what we have decided concerning your question. For it seemed good to the Holy Spirit and to us to lay no greater burden of Jewish laws on you than to abstain from eating food offered to idols and from unbled meat of strangled animals, and, of course, from fornication. If you do this, it is enough. Farewell."

Right away, the four messengers went to Antioch, where they organized a meeting of the believers and then read the letter. This made a lot of people happy because they now understood that the leaders in Jerusalem had reached an important decision. They stayed several days, and then Judas and Silas returned to Jerusalem and told the leaders how thankful were those who had heard of their decision. Paul and Barnabas remained in Antioch to assist several others who were preaching and teaching there.

෨෮෮ඁ

Several days later Paul suggested to Barnabas that they return to the cities they had visited earlier, to see how the new converts were getting along. Barnabas agreed and wanted to take John Mark with them. But Paul didn't like that idea at all, because earlier, at Perga, John Mark had refused to continue on with them. They argued, then prayed, but in the end Barnabas decided to leave Paul. He took his cousin, John Mark, and the two set sail for Cyprus.

So Paul decided to take his good friend, Silas, and with the blessing of the believers, the two men left for Syria and Cilicia to encourage the churches there.

Eight

Planning for such a journey wasn't easy. They would begin at Jerusalem, travel the well-worn road to Damascus, then generally northward through Syria until they reached Antioch. The team had friends there and it would be a good place to rest, get the latest news about the new band of believers that lived in the region. Then, they would travel along the very northeastern tip of The Great Sea and after a few more days they should arrive in Tarsus. Paul still had many friends in Tarsus and he expected an enthusiastic homecoming.

They rested in Tarsus for two days, then resumed the long walk toward the town of Derbe. Paul remembered Derbe because that was the final stop on his first visit to Cilicia. All of this was new to Silas and he marveled at his friend's memory. Each evening, around their simple campfire, Paul recounted the adventures that he and Barnabas had endured—sometimes enjoyed—while visiting these same towns. And he expected to be remembered when they arrived at Derbe because many of its residents would recall his preaching and words of encouragement.

And so it was. The Derbe townsfolks insisted they stay the night in one of their homes, a modest dwelling owned by Julia and her husband Peter Chazan, a young couple who had heard Paul preach and now were two of the leading Christians in the community.

⌇⌇⌇

Two days later they arrived at Lystra and after spending the night in the town's inn, over a breakfast of tea, flat bread and goat's cheese, Paul recounted for Silas what had happened on his previous visit.

"I'll tell you, Brother Silas, what happened to me the last time I was in this town."

"Not good?"

"No, definitely not. Barnabas and I had been preaching and teaching in Antioch and Iconium. And as we begin to do the same here, in Lystra, a dozen or so men from those two towns came rushing into the synagogue where we were about to begin. They stopped everything, dragged me out into the city square and, began throwing stones. After the third or fourth stone, I fell to the ground, unconscious. These men apparently though I was dead and they left. But—here's the miracle—God brought me back and I was able to get up and move on."

"The Holy Spirit, again?"

"Do doubt about it. I'm not certain about this, but I believe there was a young believer in that group of people who helped me. His name is Timothy and if he's still here I want to talk to him. He would be an excellent team member, if he's willing to join us."

⌇⌇⌇

Later that same day, the innkeeper told Paul that he had found Timothy and that he was waiting for him in the inn's parlor. Paul walked the few steps into the room and greeted the young man.

"You *are* Timothy, are you not?"

"Yes, Sir, I am. And I recognize you. You were nearly killed last year, by that mob."

"What brought you to that scene? You were one of only a few people."

"Sir, my mother Lois has heard your gospel message. She is now part of a small group of believing women. They meet every Sunday, they pray and the sing together. And the word is spreading. I've been a believer for two years."

"How old *are* you?"

"Just eighteen. But I've been talking to some of my friends and they, too, have accepted Jesus."

"What's your situation here? Are you willing to travel? Would you consider joining with me and my friend, Silas?"

"Yes. My mother and I talked about this very possibility. She said I should agree, if you were to ask me."

"What about your father? Is he likely to agree?"

"Yes, he is. But you should know that he's not Jewish, he's Greek."

"Hmmm, that could be a problem because the people we'll be talking to are mostly Jews and they would expect you to be one of them. That means you should be circumcised. So, if you're willing, I'll ask your rabbi to do that. We'll give you a few days to heal and then we can be on our way."

〇〰〇

While Timothy was healing, Paul and Silas explained the purpose of their mission. They told him about the meeting in Jerusalem, where the apostles and church elders had decided that the new Jewish converts would not be expected to conform to the Mosaic laws. And they emphasized that their mostly-Jewish audiences would be skeptical about this 'Jesus person.' How could he possibly survive crucifixion by the Romans? ' Did he really rise from the dead? The answer for these doubters: the eyewitness accounts that Paul and Silas had heard from those who were there. Timothy should understand that these same eyewitness were risking their lives to speak about such things. The Pharisees in Jerusalem were still very influential and their Sanhedrin council could punish anyone who spoke of Jesus as a risen Savior.

☜⟩⟩⟩⟩☞

After saying goodbye to his mother and father, Timothy fell in behind Paul and

Silas and began their very long walk northward through the provinces of Lycaonia, Galatia and Mysia. Their progress was halted only once, for several days, when they stopped in a small village. Paul told his companions that they had exhausted their meager supply of drachmas and it would be necessary for him earn enough to continue their journey.

They knew that Paul was a tent maker but they had never seen him at work. As they approached the village, Paul noticed a number of long-haired goats and he rightly assumed there should be an artisan who made cloth from the hair of those goats. He was right and the artisan gave him enough cloth for one tent. When he was finished, Paul sold the tent to one of the village elders, paid the artisan for his cloth, kept the difference and the trio resumed its journey.

As they were about to cross into Bithynia, Paul told his companions he felt that something was wrong.

"We should pray about this. I believe our Lord has something to tell us. - - - Yes the Holy Spirit wants us to go west, not north."

So, that is what they did, walking westward through the province of Mysia until they reached the town of Troas. They were dead tired and went to sleep as soon as it was dark. But about an hour after midnight, Paul suddenly awakened. He later recalled it was either a dream or a vision but he was certain he saw a man, standing at the water's edge and pleading with him to cross the sea into Macedonia. The man seemed to be pleading for help. What kind of help? The team would have to make that crossing to find out. But before they did so, they were in for a huge surprise.

☙

Paul had lost track of the man but was overjoyed to see him again.

"Friends, I want you to meet my long-time friend Luke. He's been teaching and preaching here in Troas and now he's agreed to come with us to Macedonia."

The team, now four of them, was fortunate to find a ship that was about to sail. Its destination was the small port town of Samothrace. The crossing was uneventful and after a night's rest at the local inn, the men walked on to Neapolis. It was here that Paul's vision returned. Again, the message was clear: *You are to minister to the believers in the city of Philippi. There is no church there but you will find believers who will be happy to see you.*

Philippi, Luke explained, was a Roman colony and that explained why there was no church, because the city's rulers had refused to accept Jesus. How then to minister? The innkeeper told them there was a river within walking distance and they could expect to find worshippers there, but they should wait until the Sabbath. And that is what they did.

Sure enough, there were five women, seated along the riverbank, each of them praying. Then Paul decided to speak to them. Did they know the Scriptures? Apparently not all of them. So the team spoke with each of the five, assuring them that God was listening to their prayers. One of the women, Lydia, seemed to be the leader of the group. She explained that she made a living by selling purple cloth. At this, Paul understood that she must be a relatively wealthy person, because purple cloth—most frequently worn by royalty—was intended for purchase only by those who could afford it.

After listening to her, Paul learned that she was already a believer but she rued the fact that there was no church in which to worship. Had she been baptized? No. Then, at Paul's suggestion, she called all of her relatives to the riverbank where each of them was baptized. To show her gratitude, Lydia invited the team to stay at her home.

⟳

Then, a few days later, a strange thing happened. The team was going to the river to pray, again, and they met a young woman—a slave—who was demon-possessed. She was a fortune-teller and she was making a lot of money for her masters. When she saw the men she began screaming, loudly. 'These men are servants of God and they are here to tell you how you can have your sins forgiven."

At first they didn't pay her much attention, feeling sorry for her because of the demon. But this continued to happen, same thing, day after day. Finally, Paul got tired of it all—he was quite angry—and he shouted at the demon 'I command you in the name of Jesus Christ to come out of her!' And, just like that, the demon disappeared.

But that's not the end of the story because now the slave-girl's masters had lost their source of income and they were not happy. And that's when the trouble began. Two of the town's strong-arm men grabbed Paul and Silas and forced them to walk to the marketplace where two judges were waiting. The accusers yelled at the judges, claiming, 'These Jews are corrupting our city. They're telling us we don't have to obey the Roman laws.'

The judges saw that a mob was about to grab the two offenders and to placate the mob they ordered that they be stripped and beaten. The beatings nearly killed the two men but when it was certain they would survive, the judges ordered that they be taken to the prison and kept there for as long as it took to teach them a lesson. The jailer was told he'd die if the prisoners escaped—a well-known Roman custom—and, to play it safe, he put them into the jail's deepest dungeon and clamped their feet in iron foot bracelets.

Then another miracle. It was about midnight, their first day in prison. Paul and Silas were singing hymns and praying, loudly enough so that the other prisoners could hear them. All of a sudden—no warning—there was a powerful earthquake. The prison rolled and shook for several minutes, all the doors flew open and those ankle bracelets opened.

The rolling and shaking had wakened the jailer and in the confusion he assumed his prisoners had escaped. Knowing what would happen, he decided to kill himself with his sword. Paul saw what the man was about to do and he shouted at him 'Don't do it! We're all here.'

So now, the jailer is really frightened. He doesn't know what to expect but to make sure everybody could see, he lit a lantern. When he saw Paul and Silas he knew he owed his life to these two. He dropped to his knees and asked them 'What must I do to be saved?' The answer was unexpected but life-saving.

'Believe on the Lord Jesus and you *will* be saved, you and everyone in your family.'

The jailer was so thankful that he washed away all the whip marks, being careful not to cause more pain. While he was doing that, Paul explained to him that a real believer should be baptized, not just the jailer, but his family, too.

When Paul and Silas were feeling better, the jailer invited them to come to his home. As they sat around the dinner table they talked about how grateful they were to have made new friends, friends who believed in Jesus.

⌘

The next morning the same judges who had sent Paul and Silas to prison told a subordinate to go to the prison and release Paul and Silas. They had been punished enough and they should be released. But when Paul learned of this 'offer,' he said, 'No, no, no! Your people have beaten us—without even so much as a trial—and put us in your dungeon-prison. And don't forget, we are Roman citizens! And they want us to sneak out of town without so much as an apology. You tell those judges to come here and release us.'

When word got back to the judges that Paul and Silas were Roman citizens they thought they'd probably lose their jobs. So they sent word back to the two men that they were free to leave, in other words, 'Please, Go!'

But they didn't 'go.' They went back to Lydia's home, spent the night there and reminded Lydia and her family that they should continue in their new-found faith.

ᏬᎳᎳᎩ

The next morning the team said goodbye to Lydia and began a two-day walk to the city of Apollonia. They were surprised to learn that there wasn't a synagogue in the city and a passerby advised them to continue on to Thessalonica, where they would fine one. The passerby was right and the next day Paul searched for a man had heard about before leaving Antioch. He was a Jewish convert, a man named Jason. After asking their way they found Jason at home. He welcomed them and told them they could stay as long as they wished. After Paul and his companions were comfortably settled, Paul walked to the nearby synagogue and found its rabbi.

He introduced himself, said he and his team had come a long way and would the rabbi mind if Paul spoke to his congregants? No, it should interesting to hear from a man who had traveled so far.

The next morning, on the Sabbath, Paul stood before nearly a hundred men and women. They were good listeners because it was the first time an itinerant preacher had visited them.

Early in his sermon, Paul reminded his listeners of the Prophet

Isaiah's prediction that, eventually, a Messiah would appear, that he would suffer and then come back to life. Then Paul spoke about Jesus, that his coming to earth was what Isaiah was talking about. He told his listeners that this proves that Jesus, Himself, is their long-awaited Messiah. Then he talked about the eyewitnesses who walked with Jesus, ate with him, listened to His preaching and, eventually, witnessed His death on a cross These same witnesses saw that Jesus came back to life after he had been presumed dead and placed in a tomb. And to prove He was real, he showed his followers the scars in his hands and feet, where he had been nailed to that cross.

Paul's message was so powerful and different that he was invited to preach again, twice, on the following two Sabbaths. And each time, more people came to hear him than before. After the third Sabbath, a group of citizens—including some women who were civic leaders in the city—came up to Paul and told him they had believed everything he said. How do we join your movement? Paul told them they should be baptized and later that day he led them to a small stream where he baptized them.

But not everyone accepted Paul's preaching. Thessalonica's leading citizens, Jewish men, were angry and jealous, seeing how many of their friends had believed what Paul preached. So angry, in fact, that they started a riot. The leaders knew that Jason had agreed to care for the team, so the mob attacked his home, hoping they could seize Paul and Silas and have the city council mete out some kind of punishment. But Paul and Silas were elsewhere and the rioters grabbed Jason and forced him to walk to the city council. When they arrived, they accused Paul and Silas, claiming they were 'turning the world upside down,' and causing great confusion among the people. Their main complaint, however, was that Jason—presumably a loyal citizen—had allowed Paul and Silas to use his home. And the two preachers should be considered guilty of treason because they claim that Jesus is their king, not Caesar.

The council members, after much debate, told Jason he would have to post a bond of thirty drachmas. They money would be returned to him as soon as Paul and Silas departed, assuring the people there would be no more trouble. And should the two ever return, Jason would have to provide another thirty drachmas.

⟋⟋⟍⟍⟍⟍⟍

That night the Christians urged Paul and Silas to move on to Berea, and, as usual, they went to the synagogue to preach. But the people of Berea were more open-minded than those in Thessalonica, and gladly listened to the message. They searched the Scriptures day by day to check up on Paul and Silas' statements to see if they were really so. As a result, many of them believed, including several prominent Greek women and also a number of men.

But when the Jews in Thessalonica learned that Paul was preaching in Berea, they sent some of their young men, telling them to interfere with Paul and Silas, to prevent them from preaching.

When the men in Berea learned of this, they sent Paul to the coast, while Silas and Timothy remained behind. Paul's traveling companions went on with him to Athens and then returned to Berea with a message for Silas and Timothy to hurry and join him.

⟋⟋⟍⟍⟍⟍⟍

Soon after he arrived in Athens, Paul decided to walk through the city's streets and what he saw was quite troubling. Statues and altars were everywhere, all inscribed in Greek, each one paying homage this god or that god. He decided to find the city's synagogue, perhaps its rabbi would allow him to speak to the people and if so, he would talk about those idols.

Yes, it would acceptable for him to preach in the public square.

His first encounter, upon walking through the square, was with some Epicurean and Stoic philosophers. Paul told them the story of Jesus' life and his resurrection, but they didn't believe him, thinking to them selves that 'he's a dreamer, he's pushing some foreign religion.'

Nevertheless, these men were curious enough to invite Paul to speak out publicly and the recommended that he go to the Mars Hill. There he could preach to large crowds. And that is what he did. He began his sermon by trying to flatter his listeners:

"Men of Athens, I notice that you are very religious, for as I was out walking I saw your many altars, and one of them had this inscription on it—'To the Unknown God.' You have been worshiping him without knowing who he is, and now I wish to tell you about him.

"He made the world and everything in it, and since he is Lord of heaven and earth, he doesn't live in man-made temples; and human hands can't minister to his needs—for he has no needs! He himself gives life and breath to everything, and satisfies every need there is. He created all the people of the world from one man, Adam, and scattered the nations across the face of the earth. He decided beforehand which should rise and fall, and when. He determined their boundaries.

"His purpose in all of this is that they should seek after God, and perhaps feel their way toward him and find him—though he is not far from any one of us. For in him we live and move and are! As one of your own poets says it, 'We are the sons of God.' If this is true, we shouldn't think of God as an idol made by men from gold or silver or chipped from stone. God tolerated man's past ignorance about these things, but now he commands everyone to put away idols and worship only him. For he has set a day for justly judging the world by the man he has appointed, and has pointed him out by bringing him back to life again."

When they heard Paul speak of the resurrection of a person who had been dead, some laughed, but others said, "We want to hear more about this later."

But a few joined him and became believers. Among them was Dionysius, a member of the City Council, and a woman named Damaris, and others.

⌒⟋⟋⟍⟍⌒

Paul understood that he hadn't persuaded many of his Athenian listeners that Jesus was God's son. They refused to accept his resurrection story and if only a few people believed him, then it was time to move on. He had heard much about the city of Corinth, its wickedness and corruption. Perhaps he could find a few friends there, preach and teach and make a difference.

⌒⟋⟋⟍⟍⌒

Paul was fortunate because soon after he arrived in Corinth he met two people, a married couple who had lived in Rome but had to leave because the Roman emperor ordered all Jewish people to go elsewhere. Aquila and Priscilla were tent makers, as was Paul, and they immediately liked each other, having this in common, and they decided to invite him to stay with them. (Jewish fathers were encouraged to teach their sons a trade and Paul learned from his father. Making tents was an important industry in Tarsus.)

Each Sabbath found Paul at the synagogue, trying to convince both Jews and Gentiles that Jesus is the Christ who came to save everyone, that he was crucified and ascended into heaven and is now equal to God himself.

It wasn't long before Silas and Timothy caught up with Paul and that gave him the freedom he needed to preach and testify to his Jewish listeners that Jesus is their Messiah. But some of his listeners were hard to convince, they even blasphemed and hurled abuse at the name of Jesus. After several weeks of this kind of treatment, Paul had had enough. In an angry voice he told them, 'Your blood be upon your own heads. I am innocent and from now on I'm going to preach only to the Gentiles.'

〰〰

One night, while he was asleep, Paul had a vision. It was the Lord speaking to him: *Don't be afraid, speak out, don't quit. For I am with you and no one can harm you. Many people in this city belong to me.*

After hearing these encouraging words, Paul remained in Corinth for the next eighteen months, preaching and teaching, so that many in the city learned God's truths. But when Gallio became governor of Achaia, some hostile Jews decided to challenge Paul by accusing him of trying to persuade the people to worship God in ways that are contrary to Roman law. In the court room, Paul began to offer his defense when Gallio interrupted him. He turned to Paul's accusers and said,

'Listen to me. If this were a case involving a real crime, I would feel obliged to listen to your complaints. But that's not what's going on here. You're asking needless questions about semantics and personalities and your quaint Jewish laws, so *you* take care of it. This is not my problem, it's yours. Now, you had better leave.'

But the troublemakers still weren't satisfied and so they grabbed the new leader of the synagogue, Sosthenes, and beat him up, just outside the courtroom. But the poor man got no help from Gallio who was tired of it all.

After all this trouble and commotion, Paul decided it was time to leave and go home to more familiar surroundings. He asked Priscilla and Aquila to come with him and they agreed. Silas and Timothy were ready, too. After saying goodbye to his many Christian friends, they found a ship that was going to Syria.

What lay ahead? None of them knew.

Nine

The ship's courier walked up the slope and found him in his sheltered workshop.

"Barnabas, excuse me for interrupting, but there's a letter for you. Captain Yiannis is holding it. He wants to put out to sea at first light, so you should hurry."

"Thank you, Stefan. Tell the captain I'll be there within the hour. He knows me, so that shouldn't be a problem."

Who could be writing him? Perhaps his uncle Nicos, in far-away Caesarea? Within the hour he was seated near the flickering lamp stand, with just enough light to read.

My dear nephew Barnabas. As you might imagine, news here in Caesarea travels quickly, especially when our local politicians are making that news. Your good friend Paul is here and has been for some time. I spoke with him recently and he asked me to send you this letter.

On his most recent visit to Jerusalem, Paul was accused of blasphemy by several residents of that city and for this he was put in prison, pending a trial before the local magistrate. But the prison's commander learned that Paul's life had been threatened by these same accusers. He then ordered that Paul be brought to Caesarea for his own safety and that is why he is here.

He is not in prison here, rather something they refer to as house arrest, and he's free to move about so long as he does not leave the city. He has already been questioned by two of our local governors, Felix and Festus, but no decision has been reached. There is some speculation that he may appeal his case to Caesar himself, in which event he would be transferred to Rome.

Paul asked that I be sure to mention that Luke, the physician, is with Paul. Luke is writing an account of Jesus' life and he has traveled to Jerusalem to speak with our Lord's mother, Mary.

If you are able to come, soon, to Caesarea, you should be able to speak to Paul and to Luke. Perhaps you can book passage on the same ship that brought you this letter.

Cordially, your uncle Nicos.

ᠥᠮᠥ

It was the opportunity of a lifetime. He could meet his closest friend Paul—whom he had not seen in years—and at the same time meet Luke, a man he had never met but knew much about. And if Luke had been able to speak with our Lord's mother, what a blessing that would be, to hear those stories even before they are put to parchment.

Barnabas rushed to the seaside inn, found its captain and learned that the vessel would be returning to Caesarea, first thing the next morning. Barnabas would be aboard.

ᠥᠮᠥ

Fortunately, the seas were calm, the oarsmen some of the best, and ten days later Barnabas walked ashore at the Caesarea docking station. His uncle Nicos had left him a note, apologizing for not being there, that he had a business matter to attend, but would meet his nephew at the inn nearest the waterfront, within the hour.

◈

"So, this is what my nephew looks like! How odd that we've never seen each other and our exchange of letters has only made me more curious.

"How are you, Barnabas? You look as though the voyage treated you well."

"It did, indeed, Uncle. I was most fortunate to be able to return on the same ship that brought me your letter. Tell me, have you actually spoken with Luke?"

"Yes, only two days ago. You'll like him and he'll like you, two brothers in Christ Jesus. He told me he's beginning to write his story and he's quite excited about being able to talk to our Lord's mother. But I'll let him tell you that story. I've arranged for the two of you to meet later today, at the inn where he's living. If you don't mind, I'd like to come with you."

"What about Paul? How is he?"

"He's fine. He's free to move about the city, he's been allowed to preach at our local synagogue, and he tells me some of his listeners have accepted Jesus."

"That's good to hear but I'm not surprised. Paul, ever the evangelist!

"When we meet Luke, how should I should I introduce myself?"

"Just be yourself. Luke is a very intelligent man and a meticulous historian. And, remember, he's been here in Caesarea, with Paul, for nearly two years. I'm sure Paul has told him a lot about you, after all the time you two have been together. And, another thing, in case you're unaware. Luke is a Gentile. I doubt he's ever been inside a synagogue, but that makes no difference to him. He really believes our Lord's command, that we treat others as we would like to be treated."

⌘

That same afternoon, on the inn's veranda.

"So, you are Barnabas, my friend Paul's traveling companion! He's mentioned you often enough that I feel I know you already."

"Thank you, Sir. Yes, and I've heard about your being here in Caesarea. My uncle tells me you've been able to visit our Lord's mother, Mary. Is that so?"

"By the grace of God it is. She's quite frail now, but considering her age her mind is as sharp as ever."

"Can you share some of the things she's telling you, or would that be an imposition?"

"No, not at all. I'm writing most of what she's telling me because I want other believers to know what I have learned. She understands this and has been most willing to tell me everything she can remember. That impresses me greatly, because it's been nearly seventy years since Jesus was born."

"Some examples?"

"Of course. But I should say first that many of these stories, to Mary, are quite personal and she has asked that I not include them in my written narrative. She wants me to have a deeper understanding of the kind of person Jesus was, as a child and as a young man, those years before he began his public ministry.

"To begin, she explained that her second child, James, was born just two years after Jesus' birth. As the boys matured, they became inseparable friends, even competitors in some ways. She told me that after hearing the story of David and Goliath, the boys went to Nazareth's tanner and persuaded him to make a sling for each of them. Then they walked some distance from the town's center and placed a large white stone against the base of a tree and used it as a target, so see which one would be the first to hit that stone!

"By the time he was four, his parents realized their son was very bright, enough so that Mary began to teach him to read. Mary asked Joseph if he would seek the rabbi's permission to allow her son to read from the synagogue's scrolls. This became a weekly habit and within a year or so Jesus was able to read the Hebrew texts."

"Excuse the interruption, Sir, but how did Mary and her husband deal with the knowledge that Jesus was a very special person? She knew the angel Gabriel had told her that he would be known as the Son of God."

"Yes, that is correct. The two parents were careful to treat Jesus as they would any other youngster. Of course they were curious, always looking for signs that *he* was aware of his unique stature. If he was, he never displayed it.

"Mary believes that her son had some idea of his special relationship to God but that he wanted others to see him as one of them, nothing special. That is why, she believes, that he became such a useful helper for his father, in Joseph's carpenter's shop. He worked hard at it and in his early teen years he was keeping the books for his father's business accounts.

"And he had an artistic side. He learned to draw sketches, using charcoal as his medium. Some of them were good enough that Joseph was able to sell them. And he could sing. He and James would harmonize, singing some of the ancient hymns from the Psalter.

"Then, according to Mary, Jesus realized he was attracted to several of the young women in Nazareth. At the time he was in his late teens, so it was no surprise to her that this was on his mind. He confided in her, telling her that he had prayed about it and that he was certain that God wanted him to lead a celibate life, that romance and marriage would interfere with his ministry.

"One more thing before I must leave. You know that Jesus' cousin John was a rather strange person. The two were good friends for a number of years, but then John seemed to sense a different calling from God and he all but disappeared. Years later, as you know, he began his own ministry, immersing his friends in the Jordan river and telling them they should repent of their sins. It wasn't long before he became known as John the Baptizer. And, most tragically, he eventually lost his life at the hands of King Herod."

"A nearly incredible story, Sir. Do you think your readers will believe it?"

"I do, indeed. I expect my readers to be motivated by the Holy Spirit, just as I am. And in doing so, they soon will learn to believe in miracles, as I have had to do.

"There is one other story that I should pass along. It's important to me because I heard it from two eyewitnesses to our Lord's presence *after* he was crucified."

"How could that be?"

"There were two people, Clopas and his wife, Mary. They were walking along the dusty road that leads from Jerusalem to the village Emmaus, about a two-hour journey. They had heard all the Jerusalem stories about Jesus' crucifixion and were talking about that when a third person joined them. He asked them, 'What are you discussing together as you walk along?'

"Clopas responded, 'Are you only a visitor to Jerusalem and do not know the things that have happened there?'

"What things?"

"About Jesus of Nazareth. He was a prophet, powerful in word and deed before God and all the people. The chief priests and our rulers handed him over to be sentenced to death, and they crucified him; but we had hoped that he was the one who was going to redeem Israel. And what is more, it is the third day since all this took place. In addition, some of our women amazed us. They went to the tomb early this morning but didn't find his body. They came and told us that they had seen a vision of angels, who said he was alive.

"Then some of our companions went to the tomb and found it just as the women had said, but they did not see him."

"Then this stranger replied, 'How foolish you are, and how slow of heart to believe all that the prophets have spoken! Did not the Christ have to suffer these things and then enter his glory?'

"And beginning with Moses and all the Prophets, he explained to them what was said in all the Scriptures concerning himself. As they approached the village to which they were going, Jesus acted as if he were going farther. But they urged him to stay because it was getting dark.

"When he was at the table with them, he took bread, gave thanks, broke it and began to give it to them. Then their eyes were opened and they recognized him, and he disappeared from their sight. They asked each other, 'Were not our hearts burning within us while he talked with us on the road and opened the Scriptures to us?'

'They got up and returned at once to Jerusalem. There they found the eleven and those with them, assembled together, in Mark's home. They told them 'It is true! The Lord has risen and has appeared to Simon.'

"Then the two told what had happened on the way, and how Jesus was recognized by them when he broke the bread."

"I believe this is a powerful testimony to the fact that our Lord really did rise from the dead. And I am certain that my readers will believe it."

∞

"Thank you for sharing that story. Now, what about our mutual friend, Paul?"

"Yes, I see Paul every day that I am here. He's fine, although he endured much suffering and uncertainty before he arrived."

"Can you tell us about that?"

"Yes, Paul has repeated the story several times. He wants to be certain I haven't missed anything because he expects me to write about it."

"Good, we're listening!"

"Paul had returned to Jerusalem from his third journey, this one to far-away Macedonia and Acacia. When he came into the city he had with him a man named Trophimus, an

Ephesian Gentile and a friend of Paul's who had helped him

from time to time . We must remember that during Paul's many absences, the Jerusalem citizens had lost interest in him. But when they saw him with Trophimus, some of the city's trouble-makers went to the city authorities and claimed that Paul had been seen with his friend in the temple, which, if true, would be a serious crime. Paul, of course, denied it but the crowds were so angry that they seized Paul and were about to kill him. But

by this time the commander of the Roman troops heard about the uproar.

"So the commander took some officers and soldiers and raced toward the crowd. When the mob saw the commander and his soldiers, they stopped beating Paul. Then the commander came up and arrested him and ordered him to be bound with two chains. Then he asked who he was and what he had done.

"Some in the crowd shouted one thing and some another, and because the commander couldn't learn the truth, he ordered that Paul be taken to the barracks. When Paul reached the steps, the violence of the mob was so great he had to be carried by the soldiers. The crowd that followed kept shouting, 'Away with him!'

"But the commander knew that it was his responsibility to protect Paul and he ordered that Paul to be taken into the barracks. He directed that he be flogged and questioned in order to find out why the people were shouting at him like this. As they stretched him out to flog him, Paul said to the centurion, 'Is it legal for you to flog a Roman citizen who hasn't even been found guilty?'

"When the centurion heard this, he went to the commander and reported it. 'What are you going to do? 'This man is a Roman citizen.' Then the commander went to Paul and asked, 'Tell me, are you a Roman citizen?' 'Yes, I am,' he answered.' So now, the commander is worried because he knows he's responsible for putting Paul, a Roman citizen, in chains.'"

"The next day, because the commander wanted to find out exactly why Paul was being accused by the Jews, he released him and ordered the chief priests and all the Sanhedrin to assemble. Then he brought Paul and had him stand before them."

"Paul stood and began to speak."

'Brothers and fathers, listen to me as I offer my defense.'

'I am a Jew, born in Tarsus, a city in Cilicia, but educated here in Jerusalem under Gamaliel, at whose feet I learned to follow our Jewish laws and customs very carefully. I became very anxious to honor God in everything I did, just as you have tried to do today. And I persecuted the Christians, hounding them to death, binding and delivering both men and women to prison. The High Priest or any member of the Council can testify that this is so. For I asked them for letters to the Jewish leaders in Damascus, with instructions to let me bring any Christians I found to Jerusalem in chains to be punished. As I was on the road, nearing Damascus, suddenly about noon a very bright light from heaven shone around me. And I fell to the ground and heard a voice saying to me, 'Paul, Paul, why are you persecuting me?' " 'Who is it speaking to me, sir?' I asked. And he replied, 'I am Jesus of Nazareth, the one you are persecuting.'

The men with me saw the light but didn't understand what was said. And I said, 'What shall I do, Lord?' And the Lord told me, 'Get up and go into Damascus, and there you will be told what awaits you in the years ahead.'

"I was blinded by the intense light and had to be led into Damascus by my companions.

There a man named Ananias, as godly a man as you could

find for obeying the law and well thought of by all the Jews of Damascus, came to me, and standing beside me said, 'Brother Paul, receive your sight!' And that very moment I could see him! Then he told me, 'The God of our fathers has chosen you to know his will and to see the Messiah and hear him speak.

"You are to take his message everywhere, telling what you have seen and heard.

And now, why delay? Go and be baptized and be cleansed from your sins, calling on the name of the Lord.'

"One day after my return to Jerusalem, while I was praying in the Temple, I fell into a trance and saw a vision of God saying to me, 'Hurry! Leave Jerusalem, for the people here won't believe you when you give them my message.'

'But Lord,' I argued, 'they certainly know that I imprisoned and beat those in every synagogue who believed on you. And when your witness Stephen was killed, I was standing there agreeing—keeping the coats they laid aside as they stoned him. But God said to me, 'Leave Jerusalem, for I will send you far away to the Gentiles!' "

⟨∾⟩

"The next morning the Jews formed a conspiracy and bound themselves with an oath not to eat or drink until they had killed Paul. More than forty men were involved in this plot. They went to the chief priests and elders and said, 'We have taken a solemn oath not to eat anything until we have killed Paul. Now then, you and the Sanhedrin petition the commander to bring him before you on the pretext of wanting more accurate information about his case. We are ready to kill him before he gets here.'

"But when Paul's nephew heard of this plot, he went into the barracks and told Paul. Then Paul called one of the centurions and said, 'Take this young man to the commander; he has something to tell him.' So he took him to the commander. The centurion said, 'Paul, the prisoner, sent for me and asked me to bring this young man to you because he has something to tell you.'

"The commander took the young man by the hand, drew him aside and asked, 'What is it you want to tell me?' He said, 'The Jews have agreed to ask you to bring Paul before the Sanhedrin tomorrow on the pretext of wanting more accurate information about him.

Don't agree with them, because more than forty of them are waiting in ambush for him. They have taken an oath not to eat or drink until they have killed him. They are ready now, waiting for your consent to their request.'

"The commander dismissed the young man and cautioned him, 'Don't tell anyone that you have reported this to me.' Then he called two of his centurions and ordered them, 'Get ready a detachment of two hundred soldiers, seventy horsemen and two hundred spearmen to go to Caesarea at nine tonight. Provide mounts for Paul so that he may be taken safely to Governor Felix.'

"He wrote a letter as follows:

'Claudius Lysias, To His Excellency, Governor Felix: Greetings.

'This man was seized by the Jews and they were about to kill him, but I came with my troops and rescued him, for I had learned that he is a Roman citizen. I wanted to know why they were accusing him, so I brought him to their Sanhedrin. I found that the accusation had to do with questions about their law, but there was no charge against him that deserved death or imprisonment. When I was informed of a plot to be carried out against the man, I sent him to you at once. I also ordered his accusers to present to you their case against him.'

"So the soldiers, carrying out their orders, took Paul with them during the night and brought him as far as Antipatris. The next day they let the cavalry go on with him, while they returned to the barracks. When the cavalry arrived in Caesarea, they delivered the letter to the governor and handed Paul over to him. The governor read the letter and asked what province he was from. Learning that he was from Cilicia, he said, 'I will hear your case when your accusers get here.' Then he ordered that Paul be kept under guard in Herod's palace."

⟳

"And that is how it is today. My guess is that Paul's accusers may prevail and if they do Paul is almost certain to ask that his case be made known to Caesar. That is his right, as a Roman citizen. And that would mean he would be taken to Rome for trial. Of course, if that happens I will go with him.

"As frustrating as it may be, we can only wait."

Ten

Barnabas has returned to Cyprus after a brief—but informing—visit to the city of Cyrene. He wants to tell his cousin about his experience.

⟨⟨⟨⟩⟩⟩

"John Mark, I want you to know how grateful I am that we have this time together, so much to talk about before one of us has to leave to do other things."

"Yes, Barnabas, and I know you've been busy. You told me the last time we were together that you were thinking about writing a letter, something to complement the other letters that have been written and are now with James for safe keeping."

"Yes, since we last met I've traveled south to the city of Cyrene, near the southern coast of the Great Sea. There is a large community of like-minded Jewish people who live there but I learned—after being with them for some time—that they no longer accept the teachings of Jesus and are gradually returning to belief in the laws of Moses and our other long-ago ancestors. I found this both surprising and disappointing because my Christian friends Lucius and Simeon, each of them a resident of Cyrene, had persuaded many there to accept the teachings of Jesus. In fact, they had erected a small church building and were holding worship services every Sunday morning."

"What kind of city is it, this Cyrene?"

"It's surrounded by endless desert, fresh water is always a problem, and the people who live there—understandably—feel as though the world has passed them by. That's why it's so important for them to have a faith to cling to, knowing that no matter how difficult their present circumstances, one day, in Heaven, everything will have changed to perfection."

"This letter you wrote, what was its message? You must have addressed the concerns of your readers."

"Absolutely. I wrote about the superiority of Jesus as a real person. Some of my readers are confused about that and I wanted them to understand that Jesus is superior to the prophets, superior to angels and, even, superior to Moses.

"Then I discussed what I called the priesthood of Christ, which is superior to any other priesthood, perceived or real. I mentioned that the priesthood of Jesus is superior to that of Melchizedek, the king of ancient Salem and whose priesthood, at the time, was considered superior to any other. I wrote that Jesus is God's son, the ultimate heir of all things on earth and in heaven, that He is the ultimate ruler of an imperishable priesthood of believers.

"Early in the letter I quoted many passages from our beloved Psalter, verses with which my readers are familiar. In later parts of the letter I repeated passages that were written by Moses, all of this well known to my readers. But I wanted to be certain that my readers understand that we now live in a new era and the old era, as recorded by Moses' writings and teachings, is a thing of the past. We need to look forward, with Jesus as our leader."

"In which language, Hebrew or Greek?"

"I chose Greek, knowing that many of my readers are well-educated and relatively affluent people."

"Where is the letter now, or do you know?"

"It was in the hands of the church's leader, Amazigh Albaz. He's Jewish but is now a strong Christian leader. He told me he intends to have it sent to James, for safe keeping, after he's made several copies."

"So, what's next in your busy life?"

"I've heard that our brother Timothy has been released from prison and I'm trying to get word to him to come join me, before the winter weather sets in. If he can do that, he'll bring news of our brother Paul who, I understand, is still in one of Rome's prisons."

⟨〰〰⟩

The following day, the two men met again. This time, it was John Mark's idea that the two men discussed.

"Barnabas, I've been thinking about what you told me about your visit to Cyrene. You said the citizens there are building a small church."

"That is so. Why do you mention it?"

"I've heard it said that there is another city, somewhat larger and, presumably, of more influence in that region."

"Does it have a name?"

"Yes, it was founded about three hundred years ago by Alexander the Great, hence its name, Alexandria."

"You must have something in mind, else you wouldn't be talking about it."

"I do, indeed. If there is a Jewish community in Cyrene, as you yourself have learned, it seems to me there should be an even larger one in Alexandria. What if the two of us were to go there, seek out the city's synagogue, locate its rabbi and talk to him—and others, if possible—about Jesus. We both know that our Lord told us to be His witnesses, 'to the ends of the earth.'"

"Hmmm, I believe I like your idea. But how would we get there? It's a long way across the Great Sea."

"I've already asked about that. The harbormaster at Limassol told me it's a fifteen-day journey. He said there is one ship, the largest of the fleet, that makes that trip once every month. And because the merchants in Alexandria have all kinds of goods to sell—items we know nothing about—the ship is making a good profit for its owners. Although it's mostly a cargo vessel, it will accommodate passengers."

"How do you expect us to pay for this?"

"As I've said before, my mother has done quite well for herself. I'm certain she would be more than willing to underwrite such a journey. She is a committed believer and she would see this as a splendid opportunity."

⁂

The two cousins were obliged to wait what seemed like an eternity before John Mark's mother's approval was in hand. A month later they found themselves getting off the ship in Alexandria's surprisingly-busy harbor.

"Now what, Cousin? Neither of us speaks Coptic."

"True, but I've written, in large letters and in Hebrew, a few words that should locate some kind of transport. You see, over there, a man with a two-wheeled wagon hitched to a horse. Let's go over there and see if he can help us. - - - -

"Excuse me, but can you read what I've written here?"

"Oh, Yes, Sire. I speak Coptic and Hebrew, I'm Jewish."

"Very, very good. Do you know where your synagogue is located?"

"Yes, of course. I worship there every Sabbath."

"Can you take us there, now?"

"I can do that, but how will you pay?"

"We have only drachmas, I'm sorry."

"No, no, no! We see drachmas every day. Many people from your side of the Great Sea come here."

⚬〰〰〰⚬

One hour later in the synagogue office of rabbi Aharon Brum.

"Rabbi Brum, we are John Mark and Barnabas, from far-away Cyprus, and we've come here to speak with someone like you."

"Yes, I should be flattered. What can I do for you?"

"First, you should know that we are *Christians.* Does that mean anything to you?"

"Oh, yes. I've heard about your movement, but it's far, far away from Alexandria."

"And that's why we're here. We want you and many others to know about Jesus and what He has done for us."

"Yes, well I wouldn't know about that. You probably know that we Jews are skeptical."

"Of course we understand that. But if you'll agree to hear us, we have some ideas to share with you."

"That's fine, I'm always willing to listen."

"Good. What we'll be doing his reading from the Law and the Prophets and the Psalms. You'll be familiar with those, of course. Then, we'll compare what we've just read to what we know to be true about Jesus, from eyewitnesses and others."

"That sounds reasonable, go ahead."

"You'll remember that in the first book of Moses, God said to Eve, 'You shall bear children in intense pain and suffering; yet even so, you shall welcome your husband's affections, and he shall be your master.'"

"Yes, I'm quite familiar with those verses, and many more, I might add."

"But one of our eyewitnesses has learned this: 'But when the right time came, the time God decided on, he sent his Son, born of a woman, born as a Jew.'

"That sounds to us as though what God said to Eve—as recorded by Moses—was a prediction of our Lord Jesus' birth."

"Well, perhaps; I'll have to think about that."

"Here's something else to think about. King David, in the Psalter, says this about what God told him, long, long ago: 'His chosen one replies, "I will reveal the everlasting purposes of God, for the Lord has said to me, 'You are my Son. This is your Coronation Day. Today I am giving you your glory.'

"One of our Christian colleagues learned this from a woman named Mary: She had been visited by the angel Gabriel and he told her what to expect, even though she was a virgin: 'He shall be very great and shall be called the Son of God. And the Lord God shall give him the throne of his ancestor David."

"This strongly suggests that your Kind David was predicting the birth of the Son of God, whom we know as Jesus Christ."

"Must I take your word for this, or do you have some evidence?"

"Yes, we do. It's written on a scroll which I left in the inn, for safe keeping. I can show it to you, later, if you wish."

"No, that won't be necessary, but thank you for the offer."

"Here is another passage with which you should be familiar, from your prophet Isaiah:

'The Lord himself will choose the sign—a child shall be born to a virgin! And she shall call him Immanuel, meaning, 'God is with us'.

"That same eyewitness has said this: 'Jesus' mother, Mary, was engaged to be married to Joseph. But while she was still a virgin she became pregnant by the Holy Spirit.'

"You should be seeing a pattern here. Your prophet Isaiah said a child will be born to a virgin. Yet Mary, herself, has told us how it happened: She was still a virgin when she became pregnant by the Holy Spirit. To put it another way, your prophet predicted exactly what would happen, four hundred years later!"

"Yes, I'm beginning to see your so-called pattern. What else do you have to tell me?"

"Again, it's your prophet Isaiah, talking about a future miracle-worker: 'And when he comes, he will open the eyes of the blind and unstop the ears of the deaf.'"

"And our eyewitness has told us this: Jesus told His friends to consider the miracles He was doing: The blind people He has healed and the lame people now walking without help. He cured lepers and deaf people.

"And there is more."

"Yes, I should imagine."

"You surely remember your prophet, Joel. And you'll remember his words, because you have read them many times: 'After I have poured out my rains again, I will pour out my Spirit upon all of you! Your sons and daughters will prophesy; your old men will dream dreams, and your young men see visions. And I will pour out my Spirit even on your slaves, men and women alike.'

"And, again, here is what our eyewitness has written about this: 'What you see this morning was predicted centuries ago by the prophet Joel— 'In the last days,' God said, 'I will pour out my Holy Spirit upon all mankind, and your sons and daughters shall prophesy, and your young men shall see visions, and your old men dream dreams.'

"You may not yet have heard about our belief in something we call *The Holy Spirit*, but that is what your prophet Joel is writing about when he says 'I will pour out my Spirit upon you.' In other words your prophet Joel was predicting the presence of the Holy Spirit, again four hundred years earlier.

"There is another important forecast by your prophet Isaiah. This has to do with what we Christians refer to as the 'victory over death.' And, surely, you have read this many times: 'At that time he will remove the cloud of gloom, the pall of death that hangs over the earth; he will swallow up death forever.'

"And again, we refer to what our eyewitness has written about this: 'When this happens, then at last this Scripture will come true—"Death is swallowed up in victory."

The 'Scripture' he is referring to is what your prophet Isaiah has written. So, again, we believe that Isaiah was predicting something that actually happened some four hundred years later."

"You are beginning to impress me with these writings. It's just possible, I suppose, that I could be persuaded of the reality of your Christian faith and teachings."

"We certainly hope so, Rabbi Brum. But there is one more example that you should be reminded about. It's about death and dying. And it is there to be read in your Psalter:

'Heart, body, and soul are filled with joy. For you will not leave me among the dead; you will not allow your beloved one to rot in the grave.'

"And, once more, here is what our eyewitness has written about this: In another Psalm he explained more fully, saying, 'God will not let his Holy One decay.'

"We hope you will give these examples serious consideration, Rabbi Brum. There are many Jewish people who live here, in Alexandria. It is our hope and prayer that when you share these truths with them, they, too, will consider the truths of our Christian movement. Now, it's time for us to go back to our ship."

⟨∞⟩

"The man was indeed reluctant, wouldn't you say, Cousin?"

"Yes, he was. But he *did* listen and while we were talking to him I felt the presence of the Holy Spirit, as though the Spirt was guiding our conversation, knowing that if Rabbi Blum eventually accepts our ideas it will lead to thousands of people accepting Jesus. That would mean the beginning of our Christian movement here in Alexandria and, probably elsewhere along the shores of the Great Sea."

Eleven

Finally, after more than two years, Caesar made his decision. There had been no word from Jerusalem and the emperor concluded that Paul's accusers had failed to produce credible witnesses who would be willing to travel to Rome to testify against Paul.

Paul was living in his own apartment on the *Via Calista* when he received the news. The messenger was courteous, if brief.

"A message from the palace, Sir. I believe you will find it acceptable."

"Thank you. You may go.

"Hmmm, perhaps this is what we've been waiting for. Luke went back to Jerusalem about a month ago; if this *is* good news it's a pity I won't be able to share it with him."

Paul read the scroll carefully. The writing was distinct and at the bottom he could recognize the emperor's signature under a wax seal.

"It is an answer to my many prayers, that God would have me free again. I must get word to Barnabas. The last time we spoke I told him that, God willing, I would travel to Hispania. But not by myself. Barnabas and I have walked together for thousands of stadia, preaching and teaching. We can do the same thing in Hispania."

⚬⚬⚬

Paul was obliged to wait three months before Barnabas appeared at his doorstep.

"My, I was afraid we'd never see each other again!"

"Yes, my friend. I have entertained those same concerns. It's a pity that letters move so slowly. One my father's fastest ships sailed into our harbor with your letter. I read it and went aboard for the return passage. And, here I am!

"You didn't say why you wanted me, only that it was important and, likely, would respond a new calling from God. So I'm curious, and you can't blame me."

"Barnabas, I've been here in Rome for two years and every day during that time I have prayed, and prayed; beseeching God to give me new direction. That's the reason for that letter. Our Heavenly Father wants me—and now you, also—to go to Hispania."

"*Hispania?!* A place I know nothing about. And you?"

"Yes, the Holy Spirit has assured me that there is much work to do there. The people no nothing about Jesus and many of them are pagan worshippers. The situation is similar to what we found on our first journey to Pamphylia and Laconia."

"How will we get there?"

"Coming from a ship-building family, you might appreciate the answer. Once every month, a ship with twin sails and thirty oarsmen goes from Ostia to Valencia, nearly the full length of the Great Sea. I'm told there is a decent harbor there with local accommodations.

The voyage itself may not be pleasant but once we're ashore we should be comfortable enough."

"I believe you have persuaded me. When can we depart?"

⌘

When, two months later, the intrepid travelers stepped off the ship at Valencia, they realized that no one spoke Hebrew, only the language that Paul had heard spoken during his two years in the Roman capital. He assured Barnabas that he could understand and speak it well enough.

A young man approached them, offering to carry their baggage to the nearest inn.

"How much," Paul asked.

"Only one sestertius, Sir."

"Fair enough. You lead the way and we'll follow."

"Paul, how do we manage this language problem?"

"As soon as we get to the inn, we'll learn if there is a synagogue in this city. If there is, we'll be able to preach and teach in Hebrew."

⌘

The two men were escorted to a comfortable two-room flat on the ground floor, then returned to the innkeeper's office.

"Yes, certainly there is a synagogue here. Nearly one-third of Valencia's population is Jewish. If you were to travel as far to the southwest as one can go, you would find that the town of Tarshish is entirely Jewish. You should remember Tarshish because that is where your prophet Jonah wanted to go.

"But, why do you ask?"

"We've come a long way. We're both Jewish and we'd like very much to speak to your rabbi. Do you know him?"

"Yes, indeed. We're good friends. His name is Eli Alperin. He lives within walking distance and you're likely to find him at home. If you find him, tell him I sent you."

GmmO

Before seeking the rabbi, the two men talked about how to proceed.

"What do you think, Paul? Rabbi Alperin is likely to be on his guard as soon as he learns that we're two Christian itinerant preachers."

"Yes, you're right about that. But if we approach him as we did rabbi Blum in Alexandria, he's likely to be willing to listen. Blum was attentive and he probably discussed our visit with his friends. That's the key, to persuade these men to refer to their own scriptures and then compare that to what we provide as eyewitness testimonies. And let's not forget that we have the Holy Spirit on our side. When we meet the rabbi, he'll very quickly understand that we've had much experience and are quite sincere."

"I'm hoping—as I'm sure you are, too—that he'll let us preach to his congregation. He might feel challenged to do that, after he hears what we have to say."

GmmO

The two men found rabbi Alperin in a small, dimly-lighted room, at the rear of the synagogue. He was holding a scroll in his left hand and with his right tracing its writings with a raven's feather quill.

"Excuse us, Sir. Our innkeeper told us we could find you here."

"Yes, yes, what is it? You can see that I'm quite busy!"

"We're truly sorry for the interruption but if you'll hear us out you'll understand why we want to speak to you."

"Very well. You sound as though you're foreigners and I don't meet many of those. What can I do for you?"

"Yes, we *are* foreigners. We've come all the way from Rome and our mission is to talk to someone just like you."

"In that case, let's move into that anti-room. We can sit and be more comfortable. - - -

Now, what is you want to discuss?"

"Sir, we want to be honest about this and you need to know that we are two Christian believers. It may be hard for you to understand, but we were sent here by the Holy Spirit."

'Hmmm, yes I have heard about your cult. News of this kind travels far and wide. From what I've heard I don't believe a word of it!."

"As a courtesy Sir, would you allow us to present our side of the story? You might change your mind."

"That's quite presumptuous of you, but, yes, I'm willing to listen."

"We know that you are well versed in your reading and knowledge of the Torah, the Prophets and the Wisdom literature."

"Yes. I preach from those every Saturday."

"What you may not know is that we Christians believe that

those same writings include prophesies that predict the coming of your Messiah, in the person of Jesus Christ. And we want to talk about some examples, examples that, we hope, will persuade you that this prophesies are true, accurate and believable."

"As I said, I'm willing to listen."

"Good. You'll recall that your Prophet Isaiah wrote 'Therefore the Lord Himself will give you a sign: Behold, a virgin will be with child and bear a son, and she will call His name Immanuel.'"

"Yes, I'm quite familiar with that passage."

"One of our eyewitnesses, a man named Luke who spoke to a woman named Mary, reported that Mary was visited by the angel Gabriel. Gabriel told her that she would bear a son and she asked him, 'How can this be? I am a virgin.' The angel said 'The Holy Spirit will come upon you and the power of the Most High will overshadow you; and for that reason the Child shall be called the Son of God.'"

"That is why, rabbi Alperin, we Christians believe that your Prophet Isaiah predicted the birth of the Son of God, the person we know as Jesus Christ."

"Well, I'll admit that I've never considered that possibility; your eyewitness account is something I've not heard before. What else can you tell me?"

"You may not have heard of it but there is a small village not far from Jerusalem, Bethlehem. Your Prophet Micah has written about this place in quite specific language: 'But as for you, Bethlehem Ephrathah, too little to be among the clans of Judah, from you One will go forth for Me to be ruler in Israel. His goings forth are from long ago, from the days of eternity.'

"Another of our eyewitnesses has written this: 'After Jesus was born in Bethlehem of Judea, in the days of Herod the king, magi from the east arrived in Jerusalem to inquire about the birth of Jesus.'

"To us, that means that your Prophet Micah predicted exactly *where* Jesus would be born. And we believe this cannot be a coincidence."

"Yes, I suppose if I were in your shoes I would agree with that. Anything else?"

"There *is* more. It was Moses himself who wrote 'The Lord your God will raise up for you a prophet like me from among you and from your countrymen. The Lord said to me 'They have spoken well. I will rise up a prophet and I will put words in his mouth and he shall speak to them all that I command him.'"

"Another one of our eyewitnesses wrote this: 'Therefore when the people saw the sign He had performed, the said, 'This is the prophet about whom Moses wrote, Jesus, from Nazareth in Galilee.'

"And we know for certain that Jesus grew up in Nazareth. To us this means that Moses predicted that Jesus would come into our world."

⌘

Before leaving the rabbi he told the two men that he felt he owed them an apology. He wanted some time to consider what he had heard and he thought it only fair that they be allowed to preach in his synagogue the next day, the Sabbath. Paul quickly accepted the offer.

⌘

The rabbi must have asked his followers to be sure to come and hear from this itinerant preacher from Jerusalem because in the synagogue it was standing room only. This is what they heard:

"Barnabas and I wish to thank your rabbi Alperin for granting us the privilege of speaking to you.

"May God our Father shower you with blessings and fill you with his great peace.

"Please understand that we will be praying for you and when we do that we always begin by giving thanks to God the Father of our Lord Jesus Christ.

"We are bringing to you the same good news that is going out all over the world and changing lives everywhere, when people hear it and learn about how God, through His Son Jesus, forgives each of us sinners.

"Ever since rabbi Alperin told us about you we have been praying and asking God to help you understand what he wants you to do; asking him to make you wise about spiritual things; and asking that the way you live will always please the Lord and honor him, so that you will always be doing good, kind things for others, while all the time you are learning to know God better and better.

"We are praying, too, that you will be filled with his mighty, glorious strength so that you can keep going no matter what happens—always full of the joy of the Lord, and always thankful to the Father who has made us fit to share all the wonderful things that belong to those who live in the Kingdom of light.

"For he has rescued us out of the darkness and gloom of Satan's kingdom and brought us into the Kingdom of his dear Son, who bought our freedom with his blood and forgave us all our sins. For we know that Christ is the exact likeness of the unseen God. He existed before God made anything at all, and, in fact, Christ himself is the Creator who made everything in heaven and earth, the things we can see and the things we can't; the spirit world with its kings and kingdoms, its rulers and authorities; all were made by Christ for his own use and glory.

"He was before all else began and it is his power that holds everything together.

He is the Head of the body made up of his people—that is, his Church—which he began; and he is the Leader of all those who arise from the dead, so that he is first in everything; for God wanted all of himself to be in his Son.

"It was through what his Son Jesus that God cleared a path for everything to come to him—all things in heaven and on earth—for Christ's death on the cross has made peace with God for all by his blood. This includes you who were once so far away from God. He has done this through the death on the cross of his own human body, and now as a result Christ has brought you into the very presence of God, and you are standing there before him with nothing left against you—nothing left that he could even chide you for; the only condition is that you fully believe the Truth, standing in it steadfast and firm, strong in the Lord, convinced of the Good News that Jesus died for you, and never shifting from trusting him to save you. This is the wonderful news that came to each of you and is now spreading all over the world. And I, Paul, have the joy of telling it to others.

"God has sent Barnabas and me to help his Church and to tell his secret plan to you. He has kept this secret for centuries and generations past, but now at last it has pleased him to tell it to those who love him and live for him, and the riches and glory of his plan are for each one of you. And this is the secret: *Christ in your hearts is your only hope of glory.* So everywhere we go we talk about Christ to all who will listen. We want to be able to present each one to God, perfect because of what Christ has done for each of you.

"Thank you for hearing us, may God bless each one of you.

"Amen."

CWWP

Following the service, Paul and Barnabas were surrounded by the worshippers, people they had never seen and, likely, would not see again. Nearly every one of them said they had felt the power of Paul's message and, with their rabbi's blessing, would pray that they, too, could accept Jesus as their Lord and Savior.

Twelve

The ship was two days late and Barnabas was beginning to worry. A month earlier he had received word from John Mark that he'd be arriving on *The Great Sea Explorer*, a ship that had been built in the yard at Caesarea, on orders from Rome. It was reputed to be the fastest ship afloat, with three sails and thirty oarsmen, and this would be its maiden voyage. The ship's captain, Aetius Maximus, had received orders from Caesar himself: 'Do not fail to reach Cyprus within three days, my reputation depends on it.'

It was the afternoon of the third day that the ship first appeared as a distant speck on the southern horizon, making good time with the winds at her back. By nightfall, John Mark had joined his cousin at the town's only inn. He had much to say and the telling would reach far into the night.

⟨∞⟩

"To begin at the beginning Dear Cousin, I have terrible news. I was in Rome three weeks ago and saw it happen."

"What?"

'You know from our previous conversations and letters that I've become very close to Peter. What you may not know is that Peter was one of our Lord Jesus' closest friends. He traveled with Him, ate with Him but when it really mattered, he denied he knew Jesus."

"Why would he do that?"

"What he told me is this. Jesus had been accused of blasphemy and disloyalty to the Sanhedrin—that's Israel's ruling body—and they wanted witnesses to back up the accusation. Because if their accusations were correct, then Jesus deserved to die.

"So they talked to several men, including Peter. Peter said he didn't even know Jesus. Then, a few hours later, late at night, Peter was in a courtyard warming himself by a small fire. One of the women saw him and told him she recognized him as one of Jesus' closest followers. He denied it. A few moments later another woman asked him if he was positive about his denial and he said, yes, ye was certain.

"And that's when the people in that small courtyard heard it."

"Heard what?"

"The early-dawn sound of a cock's crowing.

"And that's when Peter broke down a cried his eyes out, right in front of me."

"Why would he do that?"

"Because Jesus had told him, earlier, that by the time the cock crows, he Peter, would have denied Jesus three times. Peter knew that Jesus could predict the future.

"So, when Peter eventually moved to Rome—I'm quite certain he joined Apostle Paul at that time—he was a broken man. Thoroughly ashamed of himself and because he was so distraught he offered nothing in his defense."

"Defense?"

"Yes. Caesar's Pretorian Guard accused Peter of being one of the leaders of a new movement. They called it The Way. Caesar's top advisors considered these people a threat to the empire. They had a so-called trial, which I was able to overhear because they did it at night in one of the smaller public squares, and they sentenced Peter to death. They gave him his choice: How did he want to die? Fifty lashes, decapitation, by sword thrust or crucifixion."

"Some choice."

"Yes. Peter told them that if he had to die he wanted to die just as his Savior had, on that cross at Golgotha, just outside Jerusalem. But he said he wasn't worthy of dying that way. He told his executioners to go ahead, nail me to a cross, but I want you to turn it upside down."

"Hmmm, yes, that's the Roman way. Their cruelty has no limits."

"Exactly. I watched the entire sordid scene and I believe that Peter died within an hour. He never made a sound, but that was the way he wanted it."

The two friends decided to overnight at the inn. John Mark had more to report to his cousin Barnabas. It would take a while.

⁊⟋⟋⟋⟍⟍

Barnabas and the inn keeper had become good friends. Before turning in for the night, Barnabas reminded Adonis that it was his turn to provide breakfast. The two cousins sat at a small wooden table, savoring freshly minted tea, two slices of unleavened bread and orange juice. John Mark continued his story.

"I know, Dear Cousin, that you have been moved by our Holy

Spirit many times, especially when you were traveling with Paul. That being true, you can understand how the Spirit worked in the life of my friend Peter. I can think of several examples but one in particular stands out."

"Interesting. I'm listening."

"You'll recall that the small city of Joppa is one of Israel's two ports, the other is Caesarea. As Peter told me the story, there was a woman who lived in Joppa, named Tabitha. She was a seamstress and, apparently, a very good one. She sold garments to her friends and used the money to help poor people and she had become quite popular.

"But the poor woman became ill and she died. Several of her women friends washed her body to prepare it for burial, and laid her in an upstairs room. At the same time, two of her friends knew that Peter was nearby and they found him, explained what had happened and begged him to come to Joppa. Peter agreed and followed the friends to Tabitha's bedside. Of course, the room was crowded with mourners, many of them weeping. One of them showed Peter some of the garments that Tabitha had made for her.

"You can imagine how Peter responded to this. He asked the mourners to leave the room. He got down on his knees and prayed. Then he turned to the body and said 'Get up, Tabitha,' and, believe it, Friend, she opened her eyes and sat upright! Peter extended his hand, helped her to her feet. Then he called the mourners to come into the room and they could hardly believe what they were seeing.

"So, the news spreads like wildfire, not just in Joppa but throughout the region. Although he hadn't intended it, Peter learned the next day that dozens of citizens had become believers."

"Yes, I *can* believe that. One of our believing friends coined a new word. It's *evangelism*, and our mutual friend Peter, the *evangelist*, was one of the best."

⌒ⱳⱳⱳ⌒

An hour after finishing breakfast, John Mark resumed his story.

"You might have asked yourself, Dear Cousin, what I've been doing in Jerusalem, now that my best friend Peter has gone to Heaven."

"That would be true, yes."

"You may not have heard this but James, our Lord's half-brother, is now leading our small band of believers. It's not easy because the Romans are everywhere, searching out every home they can find, looking for our brothers and sisters. So each one of us has learned to stay out of sight and, when we can, we get together in small groups to pray and sing hymns.

"It was at one of these gatherings that I asked James if he would allow me to begin writing an account of Jesus' ministry. Peter had told me many, many stories and I believed it important to get it written down before my memory began to fail. He thought it was a good idea but he warned me that a papyrus scroll long enough for such a project would be very expensive. I reminded him that I had been living with my mother for the past five years and she had become quite wealthy; I was certain she would provide the money needed for the scroll—*three* scrolls, as I later learned.

"So, that's what I've been doing for the past year or so. Remembering, writing, remembering and writing some more. When I finished my work I realized the story had consumed some fifteen thousand words, the three scrolls being just enough."

"What happened to the scrolls?"

"James has them. He told me he knows that our tax-collector friend Matthew is working on a similar project and he believes that some day these stories should become a permanent record. Failing that, in another generation or two, no one will know about Jesus. And that is something we cannot allow to happen."

"I know nothing about writing but I do know something about telling a good story. You're expected to get the listener's attention so he'll want to hear more."

"That's true and that's what I tried to do."

"How?"

"I began by writing about John the baptizer. I knew John, slightly, but the stories about him and his ministry were known to many, so finding reliable sources was easy enough."

"An example?"

"Yes. Here's what I remember, beginning with something Prophet Isaiah wrote some 900 years ago:

The beginning of the gospel of Jesus Christ, the Son of God.

As it is written in Isaiah the prophet: "Behold, I send my messenger ahead of you, who will prepare your way.

The voice of one crying in the wilderness, 'Make read the way of the Lord, Make His paths straight.'

John the Baptist appeared in the wilderness preaching a baptism of repentance for the forgiveness of sins. And all the country of Judea was going out to him, and all the people of Jerusalem; and they were being baptized by him in the Jordan River, confessing their sins.

John was clothed with camel's hair and wore a leather belt around his waist, and his diet was locusts and wild honey.

And he was preaching, and saying, "After me One is coming who is mightier than I, and I am not fit to stoop down and untie the thong of His sandals."

"Of course, John is referring to Jesus when he says *One*."

"I agree. That's a very good beginning and any reader will want to know more. But, tell me Cousin, how are things going for you, here?"

"It's a tough go, John Mark. As you can imagine, virtually everyone who lives here considers himself a 'son of Moses.' There are now four synagogues on the island, and the rabbis who lead them are very influential men. They consider me to be a heretic, preaching and teaching about Jesus. But here in Salamis I've managed to gather about fifty people, men *and* women. We meet every Sunday morning in an old, abandoned building and the authorities—so far, at least—have left us alone. For the past six months or so we've been trying to raise enough money to put up a real church building and I'm optimistic that the project will be completed by the end of the year."

"What about ordinary citizens? How do they feel about you?"

"It depends. Those who refuse to believe my preaching about Jesus, they tend to ignore me. Those who *do* believe are my most ardent supporters. But, there's another bunch and they resent me because I'm threatening their livelihoods."

"How so?"

"It's hard to believe that in this day and age we'd still have a group of pagans, animal and object worshippers, but they're here, about ten of them. They use soapstone and carve figures of Baal, the head of a bull, and the figure of a pregnant female—that's the fertility goddess, they say. And a lot of people believe this and buy those figures in our local marketplace. I've received a few threats from them, delivered by their leader, but I tell him to leave me alone.

"But what about you? You've come a long way and you don't need to sit here and listen to all my troubles."

"Yes, and I can begin by reminding you of that long-ago time when Jesus sent us out with about seventy of His disciples. We traveled all over Judea, visiting the villages and homes where Jesus had been. It was a long, hard slog and what I remember most about it was that when we returned, Jesus told us that we should forgive those who rejected out testimony, no matter how we felt about it personally."

"Of course I remember that. It was my most memorable experience with our Lord. But why do you bring that up?"

"Because it still haunts me, something I did that I'll never forget."

"So, tell me about it."

"You may have heard parts of this story but I was an eyewitness. After having supper with His disciples, Jesus walked over to the garden at Gethsemane. He stayed there long enough to pray about what He knew was coming, namely that the Romans were about to arrest Him.

"This was late at night and I was sound asleep when one of Jesus' disciples came running up to my house, knocked on the door and told me what was happening. He said there wasn't much time and if I wanted to see it I'd have to hurry. So I grabbed the sheet off the top of my bed and ran as fast as I could. When I got there the Roman soldiers had already arrested Jesus and His disciples were trying to get away, to avoid being arrested with Him. So I decided I'd better do the same and as I turned around to flee, one of the solders grabbed that sheet and I had to run all the way back to my house naked.

"And that's what haunts me, Friend. I feel so ashamed of myself for deserting our Savior at such a time."

"Well, you said it yourself. Jesus insisted that we forgive our enemies, no mater what."

"Yes, I know that. But it's something I'll never forget. And when I get to heaven I'm going to tell Jesus how sorry I am."

꧁꧂

Some time later, John Mark returned to Jerusalem. He left this written account with James, intending that it be made part of the church record.

"I left Salamis after staying with Barnabas for two months. During that time we exchanged many stories and ideas, many of which I have written for James and the other church elders. But that record should include a description of the last days of our dear brother Barnabas. It happened this way. And I should mention that I heard this story from Barnabas' sister-in-law and I know it to be accurate.

"Barnabas' preaching about Jesus and eternal salvation was well-received by a large number of Salamis' citizens. But not all believed, especially those few pagans who made a living by selling carved images of the objects they worshipped. They considered Barnabas to be their principal enemy and their leader challenged Barnabas to stop. He said he would never stop because he knew the Holy Spirit wanted him to continue. The leader told him that was his decision but he predicted that he would regret it.

"Then, a few weeks later and at two o'clock in the morning, Barnabas realized his house was on fire, a blaze deliberately set by those idol worshippers. His first reaction was to waken his wife and get her to safety. His sister-in-law was in another room and she escaped with only minor burns. But not Barnabas and is wife. Apparently the smoke was too heavy and they were unable to escape. They both perished.

"That left it to me to arrange for a proper burial and a memorial service. I remember that my sermon said something about forgiving our enemies, but, truth be told, my heart wasn't in it."

Epilogue

A few days following Barnabas' memorial service, John Mark arranged for passage on the next ship leaving the island. There was nothing more for him to do there, the church that Barnabas had organized was growing, slowly but surely, and he wanted to return to Jerusalem as soon as possible. His widowed mother, Mary, was living alone and, as far as he knew from a long-ago visit, her health was failing. Adding to his angst was his knowledge that the Christian community in Jerusalem was being harassed by the many Jewish residents who had refused to accept the gospel stories. He knew that most of the believers had moved to Antioch which had become a safe-haven for the struggling group.

But there was some good news. He had received word from a fellow believer who recently had returned from Alexandria. It seems that a certain rabbi Blum had accepted Jesus as his Lord and Savior and his entire congregation had followed his decision. Blum described his conversion ad 'a Spirit-led Miracle.' Already the new believers had constructed their own church and were attending worship services every Sunday.

A few days later another traveler reported having just arrived from Ispania. There, in the city of Valencia, a rabbi Alperin had allowed Paul and Barnabas to preach to his congregation. The rabbi had accepted Jesus and many of his followers were doing the same.

⁐ↀↀ⁐

Some two months later John Mark arrived in Jerusalem, only to learn that he was too late. His mother had died and was buried in a cemetery plot that the small Christian community had consecrated as its own, with grudging agreement from the city's ruling council. So, what to do? He decided to go to Antioch, meet with the town's elders and seek their advice.

It was an arduous journey, some twenty days by horse cart, but less expensive than going by sea. He found what he was looking for, a modest house at the edge of the town, which James had declared to be the new Christian church's home. He stayed with James for only two days, the two of them discussing what to do next to extend the church's outreach. James persuaded him that the church's future really lay in Rome. There was a small group of believers there and Paul had written to them, a lengthy letter which James believed to be the most powerful apologetic for the Christian faith yet produced. But if the fledgling Christian movement were to succeed, that could only happen at the center of the known world, Rome.

Finding a ship to take him to Rome wasn't easy. They sailed only three times a year, to avoid the Winter storms that plagued the Mediterranean waters. But his patience had its rewards and six months later John Mark was safe and secure in the home of Tertius, a fellow believer and the man who had penned Paul's letter to the church at Rome.

⚬〜〜〜⚬

"Brother Tertius, what happened to Paul? You knew him as well as anyone."

"Yes, that is true. Paul had been under house arrest, first in Caesarea and then here in Rome, because he had appealed to have Caesar hear the accusations that had been brought against him by certain persons in Jerusalem. After about two years, the Roman authorities had heard nothing from Jerusalem and they assumed Paul's accusers had failed to find witnesses who would testify against him. So, they set Paul free and he immediately made his way to Hispania, something he had wanted to do for a very long time.

"I know nothing about what he did in Hispania because immediately after his return to Rome, the emperor, Nero, had Paul arrested. Nero said he considered Paul a threat to the empire because Paul insisted that Jesus was the only king who mattered. After no more than a few days in prison, Nero ordered that Paul be executed. A squad of Roman soldiers escorted him some distance from the city center, on the Appian Way, forced him to kneel and one of them beheaded Paul with a sword. I know that our Lord Jesus commands us to love our enemies as ourselves and I can only pray that these executioners will, some day, learn these gospel truths so that they, too, can be forgiven."

"Thank you for telling me that, Tertius. I had assumed that something awful must have happened to Paul because none of my friends had heard from or about him for a long time. But your story reminds us that Nero is a serious threat to our movement."

"That is so, but we have our ways. We meet in small groups, no more than four to six at a time, in each other's homes. There we mostly pray and sing hymns and reminisce about our lives in Jerusalem, while Jesus was still alive. Every time we meet we invite a neighbor to these gatherings, someone who knows little or nothing about The Way. Little by little we're increasing our numbers and so long as the Romans don't learn of this, some day there will be enough of us to come out of the shadows and make a difference."

"That's good to hear, Tertius. And I have a favor to ask of you."

"Please."

"Would you allow me to stay with you for, perhaps, a week or so? I want to talk to as many of your Christian friends as I can, before I return to Antioch. I have this Spirit-driven impulse to learn how our movement has made a difference in the lives of ordinary people. You may have heard that our small band of believers has been forced to relocate in Antioch. But if, when I return, I can report that you Christians in Rome are expanding your influence, that should be encouraging enough that our group might decide to return to Jerusalem."

<hr />

After two weeks of walking the streets of Rome, John Mark decided to tell Tertius what he had learned.

"Amazing, Tertius, what I've learned in these two weeks and I'm most grateful for your providing a roof over my head. You spoke of 'making a difference' and I believe you have, already."

"Interesting, tell me more."

"It's no secret to you or anyone else who has lived in Rome for even a week, what a miserable life most of your citizens are facing. The most common fear is that a fire will break out and most of the buildings would go up in smoke before any help could arrive. The streets, if you can call them that, are barely wide enough for one horse cart to pass another. And after a an overnight rain, they're so muddy that even the horses find it difficult to move. There are paving stones, of course, but they're all located in the city center, where the palace and other government buildings are located.

"Then there's the problem of clean drinking water. Some of the people, those who can afford to live on the ground floor of their building, have piped water, but this is rare. Most of the water is carried in wooden buckets from a central spring and it's often polluted enough that people get sick. When that happens and they try to find a physician, they learn that a physician's services are only for those very wealthy individuals who can afford to pay what he demands.

"I also learned that the Roman rulers have structured the payment of rents so that those who live on the ground floor pay the most, because they can afford to do so. Those who cannot, live on the upper floors, and, of course, they do not have piped water. Nor do they have adequate toilet facilities. Rather than walk five or ten minutes to a public toilet, they simply throw the collected refuse out the window and this often contains urine and feces, another source of disease and death.

"Another problem for most of Rome's citizens is coping with

the changing seasons. In summer, the rooms are too warm, flies are everywhere. In winter, people are too cold and trying to provide heat for a one-room home carries the risk of fire.

"But you know all this, don't you?"

"I do. I've been living with it all my life."

"What you may not know—and this is the most important thing I've learned—is that those people I've talked to who are Christian believers, they really *are* making a difference."

"How is that?"

"Here's one example. There's a Christian family that lives maybe a ten-minute walk from where we're sitting: a husband and wife and two daughters, four and six. The husband is a shop keeper and the wife is a seamstress. They are able to afford a two-room, ground-floor flat. The family that lives above them, also four people, are not believers and their two daughters are sometimes too sick to go to school—the polluted water problem. This has happened two times in the past three months and on each occasion the Christian family has insisted on caring for the two daughters so the father and mother can get to their jobs without having to worry about their children.

"As you can imagine, it wasn't long before the upstairs family asked why their neighbors were so generous of their time and money. And that was all the opening they needed. They immediately began to share Jesus with this family, telling them about His life and his love for all the people, no matter who they were or where they came from. They said there are many Christians in Rome who feel the same way and are doing similar things, helping their neighbors, some of whom they hardly know.

"And I spoke to another family, a husband, wife, his elderly mother-in-law and two teenage children, a boy 14 and his 16 year old sister. That's a family of five, trying to get by on the incomes of the man and wife. The mother-in-law is in her early eighties and is too crippled to walk without the aid of a wooden staff. The boy goes to school but only when he feels like it; he's a real problem, very difficult to discipline. The girl—and the family was most reluctant to tell me this—was raped a few days ago and her assailant was never found. When the father reported this to the police, they shrugged it off, saying it happens all the time and without a name or a description of the man, the police can't—won't—do anything.

"After hearing this much of their story, the wife asked me to step into another room—they live in a two-room flat, all five of them— and she told me about their upstairs neighbors. She didn't name them, and I can understand why, but she said she's learned that they are Christians, a man, his wife, and two nearly-grown children, a boy and a girl. The husband is employed in a wood-working shop, it makes chairs and tables and, yes, walking sticks. When they learned of the elderly woman's situation, he made a walking stick, just the right length for her to use. And he *gave* it to her, no charge.

"When they learned about the rape, the girl immediately went to the victim—they already knew each other, but only slightly— and was able to learn how it happened. She wanted to know if a pregnancy might be possible. No, she was certain that wasn't a problem, but over time the two have become close friends. Now they're both sharing stories about Jesus and the others in the family are beginning to see how faith *does* make a difference.

"Those are only two examples, Tertius. I can recite several others, but the story is generally the same. Christians helping neighbors, spreading the gospel message. You can believe that these stories are moving through your city like a raging fire, a fire which cannot be extinguished."

⚬ππ⚬

Historians tell us that these examples of Christians helping others are the root cause of Christianity's explosive growth throughout the Western Hemisphere. From a few hundred believers in Rome in the first century, the faith had reached as far north as the British Isles and as far east as the Volga River. In the year 1000, ten centuries after the deaths of Peter, Paul, Jesus and the others, more than one hundred million people had become believers. Today, there are more than **two billion** *of us and, by the grace of God, when the Rapture comes each one of us will be ready.*

Amen.

About the Author

John Sager is a retired United States Intelligence Officer whose services for the CIA, in various capacities, spanned more than a half-century. Like many of his colleagues he was skeptical of the Christian faith until, in his early forties, he accepted Jesus as his Lord and Savior. Since then he has been an active

©Yuen Lui Studio, 2003

apologist for Christianity, leading Bible study groups, as a lay teacher and, currently, an active participant in the BeFrienders ministry. A widower, he makes his home in the faith-based Covenant Shores retirement community on Mercer Island, Washington.

Printed in the United States
By Bookmasters